SIMPLE PRAYER

THE GUIDE FOR ORDINARY PEOPLE SEEKING THE EXTRAORDINARY

RACHEL LARKIN

Simple Prayer: The Guide for Ordinary People Seeking the Extraordinary

© 2017 by Rachel Larkin. All rights reserved.
Editor: Rebecca Hastings

ISBN: 978-0-473-39862-0 (paperback)
First Edition 2017

To my wonderful husband
And to my three awesome sons-
You are my passion and delight. I will love you always.

To my amazing parents-
Who taught me by their example to love the Lord with all my heart.

To my Heavenly Father -
May your Name be given all the glory through this message.

Contents

INTRODUCTION

Prayer is good for us. We all know this, don't we? But when it comes down to the moments in our day, do we pray? It seems that over time we have put prayer up on a pedestal and have made it more difficult than it really is. Praying to God is simple. Maintaining a prayer lifestyle is the test. How can you have a fresh and growing relationship with God amid your normal everyday life?

This book will take you on a journey to discover that prayer is not only good, but essential. You will uncover how prayer is foundational to your personal growth and how to develop your own prayer growth plan. We will explore three ways of talking with God, or what I like to call, prayer languages. These three prayer languages will unlock the secret of having a fresh and growing relationship with God whether your relationship is flourishing or failing. I have tested this approach of talking and listening to God in my own life, experiencing a deeper, richer intimacy with God. You can discover this rich relationship starting today.

I Am Not There Yet

Here is my confession: I am not there yet. I don't know all the answers about prayer. I am always learning and growing. This is a good place to be, a lifelong learner. We are all on this journey of growing in our faith, and it is good to share with each other how God is working in our lives. The older I get the more I learn about praying, talking and listening to God.

I am just an ordinary believer who has a desire to see God turn up in the midst of her real daily life. This desire to see God turn up is what has led me down a path of discovery in prayer. I have read many books on prayer and I have found it easy to become discouraged. It seems that only famous preachers or speakers and former missionaries have written books on prayer. How could I, an ordinary believer relate to their experiences? They don't have a normal nine to five job like me. They don't all have the struggles of being a mum to a family of sons.

Many of the books I have read on prayer, focus on warfare and battles. Yes, we are in a battle against spiritual forces, but a solider isn't in battle constantly. There are times in our lives that will require prayer warfare. Thankfully they are for a certain time period. Otherwise, we would be constantly on a stressful battle front alert. I wanted to learn, from everyday people, how they talk and listen to God. How do they practically grow in prayer in their normal Christian lives?

What You Will Find in This Book

In Part One, you will discover how amazing prayer is. How effective it can be. How God desires it. How you can see God turn up in your normal everyday life. Having an amazing prayer life is not for the famous Christians; it's for you and me, ordinary people who are seeking the extraordinary. You will be challenged to review your prayer life asking, what role does prayer have in your life? We will explore how you can move from wishy-washy praying to something more intentional and full of power. I will share how you can pray when life is tough so that you keep going and not give up.

In Part Two, you will discover the steps to create your personal prayer growth plan. We will look at how prayer journaling can transform your relationship with God and you will learn how to get from fig tree praying to mountain moving praying! Part Three is the secret sauce of prayer. You will discover three prayer languages or ways of talking with God. Learning how to pray using these three languages will bring your prayer life alive. You will have a fresh and growing relationship with God in the midst of your normal everyday living.

Who Is This Book For?

This book is for the ordinary Christian believer who desires to see God turn up in their everyday life. It's for those who are seeking the extraordinary and long to see God's fingerprints in your circumstances. Christians who have known the Lord for some time will discover a breath of fresh air in their prayer life, and new Christians who are wanting to discover how to pray will find this guide helpful.

FREE DOWNLOADS

To help you on your prayer journey, I would like to offer your three free downloads.

These are found on my website at rachellarkin.com/simpleprayerbonus

1. A Personal Prayer Growth Plan worksheet

2. The 3 Prayer Languages Approach - a handy one page reminder of the three prayer languages that you can print out and place in your journal or on the fridge.

3. My "12 Most Useful Books on Prayer" List

4. A short ebook "The Untold Story: 7 Steps to Experiencing God in the Midst of your Real Messy Life"

PART ONE:
How to Deepen Your Prayer Life

16

Seeking the Extraordinary

I want to see God turn up in my day. That is the main reason I pray. I don't want to be a Sunday Christian. I don't want to go through life never seeing God's fingerprints, missing how He is working out everything for good. I want to be amazed every day by God's provision, love, humor and wisdom. I want a real relationship with God through His indwelling Spirit. I want to know God for real. I don't want to live a fake Christian life.

I have come across many Christians who believe that God doesn't speak to them, that God only speaks to special people. This is so wrong. It's a lie from Satan himself. Satan is not just a liar, but the father of lies. Don't believe the lie that God doesn't speak to you for one moment. God desires to have conversations with all His children. He has no favorites. He works with His children in different ways because we are all different, right? His promises are for everyone who believes.

Every day is special and can be filled with God moments. Do you believe that? "The faithful love of the Lord never ends! His mercies never cease. Great is His faithfulness; His mercies are new each morning." (Lamentations 3:22-23 NLT). God wants to fill our days with Himself.

How to Look for God

We see what we focus on. There is an advert by the car manufacturer Skoda going around on YouTube now which illustrates this point. It shows a street with a block of colorful shop fronts and different vehicles out front. In the middle of the street is their latest blue Skoda Fabia. The commentator describes how amazing this car is, that people are so focused on it that they stop in their tracks. He then asks the question: "Did you see anything change?" Of course we say no. But as they replay the scene again we noticed that yes, the buildings have changed color, the van had turned into a taxi. While we were focused on the blue Skoda the whole environment was transforming and we didn't even realize it. Our brains were so focused on the main object, the blue Skoda, that everything else became secondary.

We noticed this phenomenon when we were looking to buy a bigger vehicle to accommodate our growing sons. We started seeing minivans everywhere. Nothing had changed. There were still the same number of minivans as before but the difference was that now my mind was focused on this particular vehicle. It is the same in our lives. *You won't see God turn up in your day if you are not focused on Him.*

In chapter 6 of the book of Isaiah, the prophet describes his encounter with God sitting on His throne. An awesome encounter giving a glimpse of heaven we would all love to have. Isaiah noted what the Seraphim were calling out, "Holy, Holy, Holy is the Lord Almighty. The whole earth is full of His glory." (Isaiah 6:3). The whole earth, which is where we live out our lives, is full of God's glory. We don't have to go far to see God's glory; the earth is full of it. I took this to heart in October 2016 and for that whole month, 31 days, I intentionally searched for God every day and wrote about it on my website. I am now beginning to recognize the eternal, spiritual world behind the temporary and physical.

Where you look is where you go. Where do I want to go in my life? I want to see God turn up in my messy real life. Every. Day. I believe that He is always there. Showing up. But sometimes we don't tune in. Isaiah 6:3 tells us that God is active on the Earth. He is always at work. Working in people. Working in situations. So if the earth, where we live, is filled with His glory then shouldn't we see it every day? Shouldn't I be able to see God's fingerprints in the earth in my messy real day?

"Jesus said to them, 'Truly, truly, I say to you: the Son can do nothing of His own accord, but only what He sees the Father doing. For whatever the Father does, that the Son does likewise. For the Father loves the Son and shows Him all that He Himself is doing.'" (John 5:19). This verse in John is quite amazing. Jesus, the Son of God, can do *nothing* on his own, only what He *sees* the Father doing. If Jesus can't do anything without seeing what God is doing then I definitely can't do anything. I also need to be *seeing* what God is doing. God is always at work – in the home, at work, on my morning walk, in my car, at the supermarket, on my website. *I will find His glory everywhere I go, if I look for it.*

The first step to finding His glory and what He is working on is to tune in. Tuning in is the same as tuning into a radio station, we must find the right frequency. Prayer is God's frequency. Take some moments before starting the day to tune in and to pray for God to focus your mind and eyes on His glory and His working in your day.

We can see God's glory and the way He works in the pages of the Bible. Sometimes it just jumps out at me and I must write it down before I forget. I absolutely love these times. But I want to follow Isaiah 6:3 and John 5:19 to see God's glory and His working in my everyday messy real life. I don't want to put God in a Sunday Church box or a Morning Bible Reading box. I want to see God's glory and workings 24/7.

Experiencing the Extraordinary in the Ordinary

God often takes what is ordinary in life and sprinkles it with extraordinary divine moments. Look at Jesus' first miracle while He was on this earth. He took ordinary water at a wedding of a family friend and changed it into the best wine that the guests have tasted. He showed up powerfully in the middle of everyday life!

Jesus was involved in many occasions of adding the extraordinary to the ordinary. The crowd was hungry as they had been following and listening to him all day. The call went out for supplies, and an ordinary boy gave up his ordinary fish sandwiches to Jesus. A prayer of thanks was said over the food. Something divine then took place. Multiplication happened. An ordinary lunch turned into an extraordinary feast for over five thousand people. This kind of miracle wasn't a one-time event either.

It happened to a poor widow and her son. They only had enough supplies of flour and oil for one final meal. Her divine moment came when she was picking up firewood in preparation for their last meal. Elijah turned up after receiving instructions from God. He asks her for some bread, the very thing she doesn't have to spare. What a dilemma! If she gave Elijah their last meal then death would be coming sooner. But if she didn't share she would be refusing to care for a prophet of God. Then Elijah gives her a wonderful word telling her don't fear, continue to do what you were going to do but give me a small portion too. Watch what happens. God will make your jar of flour and jar of oil to continue to pour out until it rains again.[1] She had to activate her faith in the promise and in God. We have to do the same. We have a book filled with promises of

God taking the ordinary and making it extraordinary. What will we do with it?

I remember a time when we had a young family and very little spare money. I prayed that God would stretch the very little that we had. I ended up calling our car *the Elijah car* because of an unexplainable situation when the gauge was signaling empty. I went to the gas station to fill the car. But to my surprise the car filled quickly and the cost was only a quarter of what I would normally pay for a full tank! It struck me right there on the pavement of the gas station that something divine had taken place. There didn't seem to be any other way of explaining what had just happened. God turned up in my ordinary life!

Sometimes we have to look at the ordinary things that we hold in our hands. For Moses that was his shepherd's rod. It was an ordinary tool for his job. God had called Moses to a big task: to lead His people out of slavery. Moses wasn't too keen on that idea. He didn't think he could do it. Of course he couldn't on his own, but "with God all things are possible." (Matthew 19:26). God's answer was, "What's in your hand? Throw it on the ground."[2] Moses' rod changes into a snake. God tells him to pick it up by the tail, when he does it turns back into his rod. Moses' simple, ordinary tool of his trade becomes the very object that helps to free two million people from slavery. His rod would be used to produce water from a rock, turn the Nile River into blood and part the red sea. All extraordinary events. *Whatever your abilities or possessions, God can use them for wonderful purposes.* Dwight L. Moody, the famous American evangelist, once said that Moses spent 40 years thinking he was somebody, 40 years learning he was nobody, and 40 years discovering what God can do with a nobody.[3]

God can also use ordinary people in His work of salvation. Charles Spurgeon, the famous preacher became saved through God's use of real, every day people. Here is his remarkable story in his own words:

"I sometimes think I might have been in darkness and despair until now, had it not been for the goodness of God in sending a snowstorm one Sunday morning, while I was going to a certain place of worship. I turned down a side street, and came to a little Primitive Methodist Church. In that chapel there may have been a dozen or fifteen people. The minister did not come that morning; he was snowed up, I suppose. At last a very thin-looking man, a shoemaker, or tailor, or something of that sort, went up into the pulpit to preach. Now it is well that preachers be instructed, but this man was really stupid. He was obliged to stick to his text, for the simple reason that he had little else to say. The text was— 'Look unto me, and be ye saved, all the ends of the earth,' Isa. 45:22. He did not even pronounce the words rightly, but that did not matter. There was, I thought, a glimmer of hope for me in that text."[4]

Charles Spurgeon become a believer after listening to a ten minute talk by an ordinary person. This man did not have a theology degree or any experience in public speaking but was willing to fill in and speak the word. The church wasn't a mega church with thousands of people. The music wasn't spectacular. There was no special power point presentation. Just a willing person to allow God to use their feeble uneducated voice. That simple shoemaker or tailor would not have realized the impact his simple message made. Charles Spurgeon has been called the Prince of Preachers. He sold fifty million copies of his sermons before he died in 1892. Today that figure is well over three hundred million copies. There are more works in print by Spurgeon than any other English speaking author.[5] An ordinary man from a tiny church had a great effect. I find that particularly encouraging. We don't need to be important, super educated or rich to make an impact for Jesus. We only need to be open to seeing God at work and willing to step up as be the ordinary vessel for God to take and perform extraordinary works.

My life is filled with accounting work, home-schooling, keeping a home, writing, loving my husband and raising our children -- all ordinary work. But when I pray over my ordinary work God starts to work in the background. *I notice moments that have a dash of the divine in them.* A conversation with one of my young adult sons turns into something deeper and hearts are affected. A 'chance' meeting with a stranger becomes a moment of extra encouragement for my soul. A morning walk generates ideas that can only originate with God. The simple act of driving to work is transformed into a sacred journey of communicating with my Heavenly Father. Ordinary people with ordinary abilities, possessions and tasks can see the fingerprints of God touch their ordinariness and create divine moments.

Take Action

Change your mind about your ordinariness. Decide to believe that God can use whoever you are and whatever you have. Spend time in discussion with God. Use the ordinary moments of your day to communicate with the Father. Have a mindful attitude about the events and people that come across your path. *Look for God in those places.* Seek His glory, it's there.

How to Pray Intentionally

What comes to mind when you think of intentional praying? It sounds to me like hard work. Is it getting up at four a.m. and spending two hours in prayer before you get ready for work? Is it booking yourself in at a monastery for a weekend prayer retreat? What about a list of prayer needs that you go through every day?

Some of these may work for some people but not so much for me. I need my prayer life to be an integral part of my everyday life otherwise I will find myself giving up, especially if it involves getting up before dawn and praying for a couple of hours. I must say that I haven't closed the door on that possibility. If God woke me up and impressed on my heart to pray for someone or something then I would do it, of course. But I want my prayer life to be my everyday lifestyle. A rhythm of living. An intentional awareness of God's presence in every moment. *Intentionally turning my thoughts towards Him throughout the day -- that's intentional praying.*

"The earnest prayer of a righteous person has great power and produces wonderful results." (James 5:16b NLT). This is my go-to verse for prayer. Some translations say - *the effectual fervent prayer*, instead of earnest. We don't tend to use the word *earnest* these days. What does it mean? It is the Greek word *energeo* which means to be at work, put forth power, to effect. Energy. The idea of something suddenly becoming energized or activated.[6] Activated is a current "in" word. We usually have to click a button to activate our subscription. Nothing is activated without the click of the button. Take a car, there is a tremendous power in the engine of a car. A car could be filled with gas and have a powerful engine but it isn't effective until someone inserts a key into the ignition and turns it. Once the engine has been activated the potential in the car is ready to be unleashed.

God intends prayers to be full of energy. They are intended to put forth power, to bring about an effect, to be effective. Prayers that Work. Working Prayers. I want to pray *energo* prayers. *Energo* prayers are not wishy-washy. They have intention. There is a plan and purpose to the praying. They aim like an arrow to their destination.

These intentional prayers make something available -*ischyo* another Greek word meaning might.[7] *Ischyo* is the picture of a very, very strong man like a bodybuilder or someone with massive muscles. A mighty super-hero. *Energo* praying produces *ischyo* power. Working prayer produce mighty results. This verse doesn't say that a little power or might is unleashed when a person prays intentionally but *polys* - much, great, large amounts of power are unleashed.

Now, doesn't dwelling on James 5:16 give your faith a shot of adrenalin? "The earnest prayer of a righteous person has *great power* and *produces wonderful results.*" (*emphasis mine* NLT). A prayer that intentionally seeks for God's intervention produces a forceful power to be unleashed. This is not praying to check-off boxes. This is intentional praying, a powerful tool with great impact. This type of prayer is intended to have an effect. Most of the time we pray but we don't really believe that our prayers will have any effect. We must become more intentional in our praying. Intentional prayers get results because they have faith behind them.

How Do You Become Intentional?

Immersing yourself in the Word and discovering who God really is inspires intentional praying. Discover how other people in the Bible have prayed and what the results were. Believe in your mind and heart that God is listening. God is interested and cares about what concerns you. Believe that if you ask anything in the name of Jesus, God hears and is at work.

We must stop looking at the visible world around us and believe that as soon as you pray things are happening in the spiritual world even though we can't see it. Believe that what is spoken will eventually reveal what is happening in the invisible world and make it visible. The very creation of heaven and earth was made by words. "By faith we understand that the universe was created by the Word of God, so that what is seen was not made out of things that are visible." (Hebrews 11:3). We are made in the very image of God, having the same ability to speak Gods words allowing the invisible to become visible. That is exactly what having faith is. Hebrews 11:1 says, "Faith is the confidence that what we hope for will actually happen; it gives us assurance about things we cannot see." (Hebrews 11:1 NLT).

What is the result of an intentional prayer according to James 5:16? *It has great power and produces wonderful results.* Another word for power is force. There is a force that is released when you pray. It is not just a small force but a mighty one as defined by Greek word *polys.* With this understanding, we can rethink James 5:16 as: a seeking-after-God prayer, with the intention of having an effect, produces a strong force to start working out your request.

Start a Habit of Having a Conversation with God All Day Long

One book that is a must read for anyone wanting to develop a lifestyle rhythm of intentional prayer is The Practice of the Presence of God by Brother Lawrence. A French monk in the 1600's, Brother Lawrence worked in the monastery's kitchen as a cook despite being lame and in pain from a war injury. Even though he had a low position he was highly regarded because of his personal relationship with God. After his death, his conversations and letters were recorded and his book was published. You can find it for free on the Internet, including as a free audio, and be encouraged in your prayer journey.

In his book, Brother Lawrence explains how to start the practice of the presence of God in his first conversation with Mr. de Beaufort: "That in order to form a habit of conversing with God continually, and referring all we do to Him; we must at first apply to Him with some diligence: but that after a little care we should find His love inwardly excite us to it without any difficulty." In modern English, a praying lifestyle starts with us forming a habit, intentionally, of consulting with God in everything we do in our day. This habit needs to be practiced just like any new habit. If I want to lose weight I must introduce some new habits, like tracking my daily calories. This needs to be done on a consistent basis until it becomes a natural activity like brushing your teeth. Once this habit of talking with God about everything and anything is happening daily, it becomes second nature, and we find we are experiencing His presence without effort.

Start a Habit of Pondering God's Words

What I have found to have the most impact on my prayer lifestyle is meditating on the Word. *Meditation on God's word warms my heart and makes it ready for prayer*. I will share more on how to do this in Part Three: The 3 Prayer Languages where I talk about Praying the Word. It is normally just one verse that I am pondering, soaking all the juice out of the words. As I am thinking and turning the words over in my mind I naturally turn my attention to God and start talking to Him about the words. Asking Him to show me the truth of the words and for the words to become reality in my life. John Piper says, "The Word of God inspires prayer."[8] I have found that to be true in my life. The Bible is the very words of God. That means pondering a verse is listening to God, the very act of praying. There is something inherent in God's words that propel us to respond by talking with God.

What Role Does Prayer Have in Your Life?

What role does prayer have in your life? This is an interesting question and one that we probably should stop and ponder for ourselves. I have been challenged this year to deepen my prayer life, talking and connecting with God from many directions. My pastor began increasing prayer in staff meetings and encouraging prayer in his sermons last year. I see a difference in the pastoral staff and in the activities of the church and I believe prayer made that difference. I have felt the tugging on my heart with verses on prayer, articles and books on prayer coming across my path. The more I ponder prayer and experience regularly conversations with God the more I become convinced of the importance of prayer. Prayer is essential for all spiritual growth.

Billy Graham was quoted as having a few regrets. If he could do his life over he would have preached less and prayed more. "I have failed many times, and I would do many things differently. For one thing, I would speak less and study more, and I would spend more time with my family. I would spend more time in prayer not just for myself but for others. I would spend more time studying the Bible and meditating on its truth, not only for sermon preparation but to apply its message to my life."[9]

All good marriage counsellors agree that healthy communication is the key to a lasting and joyful relationship. Why do we think that it is any different to our relationship with God? Most believers have either no communication with God or only a one-way communication. But a deep, joyful, and satisfying relationship with God has two-way communication and prayer is prioritized as essential.

I don't want to live with regrets. According to Billy Graham, he would not regret time spent in prayer. This challenges me in three areas, to pray more for people, to pray before every activity and to pray before reading my Bible.

Pray More for People

I'm not talking about a quick – "Please God bless my sons today..." This is more in depth, asking God what to pray first and following the Spirit's lead, asking God to show me what He wants me to pray from His word on behalf of people. To do this daily and be committed to pray for people. This includes random people that I pass on the street. I could be the only person in their life that spoke to God on their behalf, what a privilege and what a responsibility. "I urge you, first of all to pray for all people. Ask God to help them; intercede on their behalf, and give thanks for them." (1 Timothy 2:1 NLT).

Pray Before Every Activity

God wants to be involved in our whole life not just our morning devotions or church on Sundays. This includes our day jobs, household chores, our leisure time, exercise time, our eating, our going in and going out. Jesus tells us to love God with everything, all of our heart, mind, soul and strength.

"Commit everything you do to the Lord. Trust him, and he will help you. He will make your innocence radiate like the dawn, and the justice of your cause will shine like the noonday sun." (Psalm 37:5-6 NLT).

This involves creating a new habit of deliberately stopping before the start of a new activity in your day and committing it to the Lord. What are we saying if we don't do this? That we are more able to carry out our day's activities without referring to Him, the creator and sustainer of life? The very breath in our lungs today is supplied by the hand of God. Let's show that by praying continually.

Pray Before Reading/Studying the Bible

Oh boy, has God convicted me on this one. I love studying the Word; it's my way of worship to God. But I have neglected to pause before I read and ask for God's direction, for God to open up His Word and my eyes to see His ways and His truth. I am currently reading "Releasing the Rivers Within" by Dwight Edwards and he says, "When we read our Bible without pleading for the Spirit's illumination, we betray a lingering confidence in our flesh that we can understand God's eternal truths through the medium of our finite, earthbound minds."[10] These words are so true. By not praying first I am saying that I can understand God's truth without the need of the Holy Spirit who God placed inside me to help me understand His truth. How arrogant!

Since increasing prayer in these three areas, I have experienced more aspects of God such as:

- An increased sense of the holiness of God. The more I pray and seek God's face the more I come away undone. I get a glimpse of Moses' feelings as he took off his sandals and stood on holy ground in front of the burning bush. This heightened sense of God's holiness seeps into all areas of my life, and it motivates me to root out thoughts and activities that God doesn't want me to be a part of.

- An awareness of God's hand in circumstances. There is an enlightenment, "the eyes of my heart have become more enlightened." (Ephesians 1:18). I can 'see' or recognize God more in the circumstances of my day. This makes for a more fun-filled and satisfying life.
- My everyday life becomes worship. Every time I talk to God before a daily activity I am putting Romans 12:1 into action. As I present my body or activity to God it is like a living and holy sacrifice.

- Increased vision. The more I pray for people the more I have to pray. God shows me more of His vision for the people that I am praying for, giving me more to pray. So exciting!

God is always wanting to take us deeper, but we have a choice. It's up to you. Are you up to the challenge? Does it go beyond something you want to try out for a while to be a lifestyle upgrade?

Don't Give Up

How do you pray when you want to give up?

"Don't quit in hard times. Pray all the harder."
(Romans 12:12b MSG).

"Persist in prayer." (Romans 12:12 NET).

Don't give up praying, even when times get tough.
When things get rough that is the exact time to dial
up the prayer, to move it up a notch and not give up.
That is what the passage in Romans 12 is telling us
to do. When life throws us a curve ball (and if it
hasn't happened yet, it will) we tend to shut down
spiritually. We dry up. We stop attending church.

The Bible gathers dust beside the bed. Praying ceases. In fact it is probably the first thing that falls by the wayside in both good and bad times.

But that is not the time to give up. It's the time to buckle down and double up on prayer. The Greek word, *proskartereo* used in this verse fascinated me. It means to be devoted to something, to give unremitting care to a thing and to persevere and not faint. To stick to something and stubbornly continue in it.[11] The question that I ask myself is do I pray that way?

This type of prayer life sounds more like a prayer lifestyle. A constant awareness of God's presence in your life. A rhythm of communicating with your Heavenly Father throughout the day. How do we create such a prayer rhythm? In one word: priorities.

I have discovered that my goals are achievable by rearranging my priorities. Last year I made my goal to lose weight a top priority in my life. For it to be the most important thing I had to rearrange my day so that a daily walk happens. I had to put in place new habits of drinking more water and entering my daily calories. And I had to do all of this without fail.

For prayer to become the rhythm of our days, we need to rearrange our priorities. It's a mental shift to be devoted to prayer. That shift happens when we believe in the benefits of what we are being devoted to. I knew with my weight loss goal that the benefits would be worth implementing the new habits in my life.

It's the same with prayer. The benefits are out of this world. God turns up in your day. Things start to work together for good. (Romans 8:28). Peace comes in and sets up guard over your mind and emotions. (Philippians 4:6-7). Relationships can be healed. Miracles take place.

How Do You Prioritize Prayer?

Here is my easy way of developing a prayer lifestyle: *Bookend your day with prayer.* What do I mean by Bookend? Start the day with prayer. The minute you open your eyes: *God, hi - thanks for the sleep last night. Thanks for being my God. Help me today with...* Then bookend the end of your day by falling asleep thanking God for the day. It's a simple but a powerful habit. It's the first habit that transformed my prayer life to becoming a prayer lifestyle where God becomes real in my daily moments.

Start Bookending your day with prayer today. Then follow it up tomorrow until it becomes part of your routine. You will find that it leads to a God consciousness throughout the day. You will become more aware of God working in your encounters with people. Life becomes an adventure and miracles may happen.

Don't Wait until You Are Perfect

Don't wait until everything is perfect before you pray. I used to think, when I was younger, that I had to be perfect before I approach God with any request. What a lie that is! Paul tells us that it was when we were sinners that Christ died for us, not when we become perfect.[12] The problem with this negative thinking is that we waste time waiting until we are perfect and perfect never arrives. In the meantime, we live in guilt and prayer is put back up on the shelf, probably next to the Bible. Please don't wait until you think you are agreeable to God; He wants to hear from you however you are.

I love how the writer of the book of Hebrews spells it out, "Let us come boldly to the throne of our gracious God. There we will receive his mercy, and we will find grace to help us when we need it most." (Hebrews 4:16 NLT). Just before this verse the writer tells us the reason we can be so bold: we have a High Priest who understands our weaknesses. He is the one who goes before us so that we can boldly enter God's presence. Rick Renner in his book <u>Sparkling Gems from the Greek</u> explains this verse well, "This verse says that we are to come 'boldly unto the throne of grace.' The word "boldly" vividly portrays how much God wants you to come to Him, for it is the Greek word *parresia,* which gives the idea of *boldness, frankness, forthrightness,* and *outspokenness.* This clearly means God wants you to be very direct about telling Him when you need help! You never have to be timid or fearful about telling the Lord exactly what you are facing and what you need, because he encourages you to speak up and be bold!"[13]

Change Your Mindset

Develop a mindset that constantly refers to God, in effect practicing the presence of God. We naturally think of ourselves in tough situations but the next time you find yourself facing a problem, big or small, train your thoughts to turn to God in prayer. It takes time and practice to develop this mindset. As you repeat the cycle of placing your focus on God in these times it will become automatic. One of my favorite Psalms is Psalm 46. "God is our refuge and strength, a very present help in times of trouble." (Psalm 46:1). Think on this verse for a moment. God, the creator of everything we see, can be our strength and our help. Why do we not turn to him instantly? We have such a large reservoir of help and strength that we are not connecting to on a regular basis. I am writing this to myself as well as to you. I think we miss out on so much inner strengthening from God to face the big and small things in our lives.

Take Action

After you finish reading a passage of scripture see if you can turn it into a prayer. Talk to God about what you have read. Is there something that you don't understand? Ask Him. Is there something that you can declare aloud about your situation or about God? Speak it out. Is there something lacking that the scripture pinpoints? Request God to fill your lack. Don't just read the word; soak it in prayer until it becomes part of who you are.

PART TWO:
Creating a Personal Prayer Growth Plan

How to Create a Personal Prayer Growth Plan

"Change is inevitable, growth is optional."

-Dr John C Maxwell

Recently I realized that I have a growth plan in many areas in my life-

- I have an eating plan to maintain my weight.

- There is my walking program to keep healthy and fit.

- We have an ongoing program to declutter our home.

- I have a reading program to satisfy my

passion for learning.

These are all designed to improve myself in these areas. They are growth plans and they are effective. But do I think about growing in Prayer? Do I have a Prayer Growth Plan?

John Maxwell led an on-line seminar recently and he made the point that we should plan for personal growth. Growth is not automatic. "If you are going to grow you have to be intentional...you have to grow on purpose."[14] When I heard him say that it made me think about the areas of my spiritual life that I need to grow on purpose. Prayer is one area that seems to always need work, doesn't it? To me, Bible study seems easier. We can touch and read something tangible. But prayer can seem to be talking into thin air. As I have travelled on my personal prayer growth plan, **I have discovered prayer to be the very air that we need to breathe to see the extraordinary.**

This growth plan is an active process that develops as we walk with the Lord just like a healthy father/son or daughter relationship deepens as time goes on. It is not a set of rules or a program to follow but the deepening of a relationship. Its focus is on God and His Son, Jesus through the workings of His

Spirit that lives inside us not on what we can get from our praying.

Our relationship with God is vitally important, more so than our plan to lose weight or declutter our home. Why do we not treat our spiritual life with more thought than the rest of our life? It comes down to what we consider to be of utmost importance.

Take Action

Are you willing to do what it takes to make prayer a priority and create your personal prayer growth plan? Watch the YouTube video of John Maxwell explaining the importance of planning for growth.

What Is Your Focus for Growth?

"It is not the number of books you read, nor the variety of sermons you hear, nor the amount of religious conversation in which you mix, but it is the frequency and earnestness with which you meditate on these things till the truth in them becomes your own and part of your being, that ensures your growth."
-Frederick W. Robertson

Prayer plus the Word are the foundation for any sort of spiritual and personal growth. It says in Psalm 1 that the person who meditates on God's word day and night is like a tree that yields fruit. That is the growth we are looking for. People tend to gloss over the meditating part and take that to mean just reading of the Word. But meditating includes prayer, talking to God about what is written. I learn and grow when I take one verse, ponder on it, pray on it and act on it. Word plus prayer is super growth. Beth Moore agrees in her book <u>Praying God's Words</u> where she says, "I am utterly convinced that the two major weapons with divine power in our warfare are the Word of God and Spirit-empowered prayer."[15]

Our motivations are most important. Behind all the reading, meditating and praying is the desires or intentions of our heart. What is our intention for spiritual and personal growth? Recognition? Knowledge? A sense of making it or being further down the track than others? Could it be comfort in knowing that you are ticking all the right boxes? Beth Moore hits the nail on the head when she says, "Without a doubt, prayerless lives are powerless lives, and prayerful lives are powerful lives: but, believe it or not, the ultimate goal God has for us is not power but personal intimacy with Him."[16]

In our prayer life we need to be seeking the Provider and not just what He provides. In our reading of the Word we need to seek the Wise One and not just the knowledge that He gives. This is why Jesus called Himself the way, the truth and the life. He is the actual way to everything in our lives. He is the truth in every situation. He is the very life of everything. The book of Colossians explains how all things were created by Him and in Him all things are held together.

What are you truly seeking? God or ticking boxes? Or even growth for growth's sake? When we focus on the Lord we will grow spiritually and personally.

Decide and Plan

In order to grow your prayer life there are a couple of essentials that are needed. The first, as mentioned previously, is your intention. Why do you want to grow your prayer life? Make sure that getting to know God for yourself is the goal and not what He can provide or how He can change the circumstances or people in your life by praying. If your intentions are in the right place, what is next?

Decision Time

With any desired change a decision is needed. A firm commitment to the desired change is required. You need to decide that prayer and connecting with God on a daily, moment by moment basis is important to you, and you are committed to personally grow in that area. I have found that nothing changes in my life without a decision made to change and a commitment to see that change through. This will mean a change of priorities. It will mean a change in mindset. What you now regard as important to achieve in a day needs to change to include communicating with God on a regular basis.

In order to successfully make any decision you need to know why you are making the change. Why do you want to grow your prayer life? Hopefully Part One of this book has shed some light on that for you. If not, go back and reread it. My reason to grow spiritually is to see God turn up in my daily life. I want to see Him working things out for His purposes. I want to recognize His fingerprints on my life. To do that I need to be communicating and looking out for Him. It's an exciting journey.

Plan Your Prayer Growth

One of the main reasons that nothing changes, besides not making the decision to grow, is a lack of planning. To successfully change your daily life, you need to be intentional about growth. Being intentional means planning. When I was losing weight, I had to plan what I was eating and how I was going to exercise. The weight wasn't going to just fall off me. I had to plan it to lose it. It is the same with learning how to connect with God. You have to decide to do it and then plan it into your day. Don Piper encourages us to plan our prayer growth.

"Unless I'm badly mistaken, one of the main reasons so many of God's children don't have a significant life of prayer is not so much that we don't want to, but that we don't plan to. If you want to take a four-week vacation, you don't just get up one summer morning and say, 'Hey, let's go today!' You won't have anything ready. You won't know where to go. Nothing has been planned.

But that is how many of us treat prayer. We get up day after day and realize that significant times of prayer should be a part of our life, but nothing's ever ready. We don't know where to go. Nothing has been planned. No time. No place. No procedure.

And we all know that the opposite of planning is not a wonderful flow of deep, spontaneous experiences in prayer. The opposite of planning is the rut. If you don't plan a vacation, you will probably stay home and watch TV. The natural, unplanned flow of spiritual life sinks to the lowest ebb of vitality. There is a race to be run and a fight to be fought. If you want renewal in your life of prayer, you must plan to see it."[17]

Developing a plan for growth in your prayer life is a personal journey. As you embark you will discover how you relate best to God. Here are some ideas from my journey to get you started.

- **Invest time every day for connecting with God**. Sounds simple and makes sense. I am not one to get up at 4 a.m. and spend two hours praying. I have tried it and it's not for me. That's ok. I think God is more interested in our heart than our sacrifice. Take the Pharisees. Jesus called them out on their loud long public prayers because it was all for show and not with the intention of connecting with God. It was a ticking the box activity. We don't want to tick boxes; we want to meaningfully connect with God daily. I intentionally take the first moments that I am awake to talk to God about the day and I intentionally take the last moments of my day to thank Him and talk over the day's events. It's simple. Nothing over the top or complicated. But is a decision and commitment to do that every day.

- **Practice praying through the day.** My goal is to get to the place where my mind and heart automatically reaches out for God seeking

His thoughts on whatever is going on in that moment. My desire is to live, breathe and operate in His presence throughout the day. To do what Brother Lawrence did and practice the presence of God daily. Instead of just walking or exercising, add praying as well. Try adding prayer and getting to know God in your morning commute to work. Why waste that time on listening to the radio?

- **Read about prayer.** There is always more to learn about prayer. Never give up learning. Read what others have discovered in their prayer lives. There are a number of books written about prayer over the centuries. Pick twelve of them and read one a month for a year. If you are not sure on what books are worth reading I have a free download available on my website for readers of this book. (rachellarkin.com/simpleprayerbonus)

- **Research Verses.** When you have a need or an area in your life that you wish God to work on take some time out to research what God says in His Word. Remember the Word plus prayer is powerful and will super boost your spiritual growth. By writing down in your journal God's heart on what you are praying for, your prayers are targeted and will produce results.

- **Actively watch for God's response to your prayers.** This is the fun adventurous part. God wants to work in your life and through your life. Most of the time our lives just flow along without us being aware of God's actions. We may even pray for a need and then don't even recognize that God has answered! Actively watching throughout the day is essential to your personal growth prayer plan. This also involves listening to the Spirit that is dwelling inside you. He will impress on you different notions and ideas that will bring you wisdom for a particular situation or answers to problems. If you are unsure whether the impression is of the Spirit ask God. *God is this notion or idea from you? Please confirm it to me.* Don't be scared to ask for a confirmation.

- **Share what God is doing in your life.** Any outcome in our growth needs to be shared. God wants us to be a river that is flowing out to others. He doesn't want us to be like the Dead Sea where we keep all His good things to ourselves. By sharing we cement in our own minds and hearts what God is doing in our lives. It helps our faith and builds up the faith of the people we share with. Hearing how God is working in someone's life is inspiring and helpful.

Start Small – Fig Tree Praying

It's easy to get discouraged in prayer, isn't it? We question whether God is listening or acting on our behalf. Don't feel discouraged. I discovered that it is ok to start small; we all must start somewhere. In fact, God knows that it is a process. When that 'somewhere' is practiced daily it becomes 'something.' It changes from 'fig tree' praying to 'mountain moving' praying.

Fig Tree Praying – God, Please Show Up Today

That is what happened to Nathanael in John chapter one. He was sitting under the fig tree, probably praying for the Messiah to turn up (according to the scholars). This is an awesome prayer request, and it is what I pray for most days. *God, please turn up in my messy real life today. Show me that you exist. Show me that you are in the middle of the messy details of my life.*

I dare you to practice praying this. But make sure that you remain watchful during the day for God's fingerprints. They will be there. God will turn up, just like he did for Nathanael, which completely freaked him out. Check out John 1 and see how Jesus met Nathanael where he was at. Just sitting under the fig tree asking for the Messiah to turn up.

No one knew where Nathanael was or what he was quietly praying under that old fig tree. But Jesus knew. And Jesus knows what you prayed this morning. He knows what you prayed before you went to sleep last night. He knows your deepest cry that you haven't even voiced yet. He knows. He can show up in your day today. Just ask him to, like Nathanael did.

That is your starting place: asking God to turn up. That was Nathanael's starting place. Your Prayer Growth Plan starts with you asking God to show up in your day. To make you more aware of His presence. More conscious of His light and truth in your daily dealings. It's an opening up of a daily dialog. No pressure, just talking to your heavenly father. Try it.

Don't be surprised if God encourages you to move on from your starting place. After Nathanael exclaimed amazement at Jesus' knowing what he was doing Jesus said, *that's nothing! You will see greater things than this.* (John 1:50, *paraphrase mine*). Greater things is the 'something.' We start 'somewhere' -- maybe under a fig tree. Then God encourages us by showing up in our day which spurs us on to greater things.

Fig Tree Praying – God, Please Remove This Useless Fig Tree

There was another story that involved a fig tree and prayer in Matthew chapter 21. Jesus got annoyed at a fig tree that had no fruit. He cursed it and it died suddenly. The disciples were amazed when they passed the fig tree again. Jesus was showing them the power of asking for something to be removed, something small and insignificant like an unfruitful useless fig tree. Jesus considered this level 1 on the Prayer Growth Plan. Fig Tree Paying.

Do you have anything small that is taking up space in your life? Something useless but it is cluttering up your life? It could be a sin. It could be a bad friendship. Maybe it's an activity that is not the best for you right now. Maybe certain tv shows? Maybe it's time for a fig tree prayer like the one Jesus modeled in Matthew.

Mountain Moving Praying

Fig Tree Praying is a good starting place, but it doesn't end there. As always Jesus wanted his disciples to grow. He promised that if they add faith with no doubting to their prayers they will move mountains.

And Jesus answered them, "Truly I say to you, if you have faith and do not doubt, you will not only do what has been done to the fig tree, but even if you sat to this mountain, 'Be taken up and thrown into the sea,' it will happen. And whatever you ask in prayer, you will receive, if you have faith." (Matthew 21:21-22).

This is the promise of more. The upward turn in your Prayer Growth Plan journey. Keep talking with your Father in heaven during the moments of your day. Keep watching for His fingerprints. And when the mountain moving opportunity comes along your faith will be strong.

Prayer Journaling

Most of you would probably think that I am going to teach you how to set up a prayer journal, encourage you to write long lists of prayer requests with space beside to note the answers. Maybe even include some arty-crafty journaling to bring some color to your pages. And maybe that works for you. But that is not the kind of prayer journaling that I love to do. I am a lists person and I have tried to set up such a prayer journal but there is something clinical about it. I don't want to treat God as some sort of magic genie bottle where I list all my needs and voila, the answers appear.

What I want to introduce to you is a way of recording how God is working in your life. We can all see God turn up in our days. You may feel like He is distant right now but you can know God is turning your ordinary details of your life into an extraordinary experience. We just have to train ourselves to look for Him, to expect Him, to talk to Him and listen for His reply. Our prayer journey is like a road trip. On a road trip there are markers to signify changes in the road, attractions coming up, rest stops and dangers. It is the same with our prayer journey and our life in Christ. There are markers along that way that signify an encounter with God, an answer to prayer or a seemingly amazing coincidence that was really God ordained. "Aha" moments or thoughts that are placed there by God. God speaking to you through a sermon, book or conversation. God revealing more of Himself through your interaction with nature. These markers need to be written down. They need to be celebrated and remembered.

How to Journal

Prayer is two-way communication with God. Listening and talking are the two ways. **Journaling is recording my listening and talking to God.** Journaling is documenting a person's growth journey whether it is in personal development, goal setting and achieving or spiritual growth.

Journaling is very personal and, at a glance, my journals look messy and jumbled but as you stand back and review a year's journaling you start to see a pattern or theme of progress and growth. My journals describe my spiritual life. They are a running commentary of my relationship with God.

What I want to record in my journal is my daily interactions with God, what I have heard Him say to me through His word, through nature and through what others have said. God speaks in more than one way, and I want to keep a record of what He is saying to me. Why? I am forgetful. What I have found in my journaling life is that God will lead me on a journey, sort of like what the Israelites went through in their 40 year walk through the wilderness. God will speak into my life, and I will learn valuable lessons which I quickly forget and go my own merry way. **If I have a record of God's message for me I can regularly review and make corrections in my life to match with God's message and purpose for me.**

I also record any verses that God has highlighted to me to pray for myself or others. This is invaluable in boosting my prayer time with God. If I have an arsenal of verses that reveal to me God's will in a situation I am confident in what I am praying. This enables me to pray with a heart full of faith. Regarding praying in faith, James says, "But let him ask in faith, with no doubting, for the one who doubts is like a wave of the sea that is driven and tossed by the wind. For that person must not suppose that he will receive anything from the Lord; he is a double-minded man, unstable in all his ways." (James 1:6-8). I do not want to be unstable or double-minded. The results are catastrophic: receiving nothing from God! How can we live a thriving growing Christian life without receiving anything from God? There would be no life. Jotting down verses that are applicable to what I am praying and then praying the scripture is vital and powerful. There are some helpful ideas on using Scripture in your prayers in the final section of this book, Praying the Word.

What You Will Find in My Journal:

- Verses -- Bible verses that I am praying for a need that I have

- Verses for others -- Bible verses that I am praying on behalf of someone else

- Vision -- A vision that God has given me for that year. For 2017 my vision was:

"This is the Year!
to listen to the Spirit of God,
to be unleashed in a sea of His love,
to live & breathe the Kingdom
TRUE FREEDOM
to love without limits
to visit the broken with God's unlimited love
to see God working
to pray effectively
to live worshipfully
to speak grace words
This is the Year!"

I have this printed on an image and pasted into the front page of my current journal. I regularly read it out loud and remind myself of the areas where God wants to carry out His sanctifying work.

- Daily Declarations -- Statements of truth that I declare over myself regarding my work, spiritual life and my family

- My One Word notes -- Every year I ask God for a theme or One Word that He wants me to focus on for that year. I have written an article about this on my website.[18] My journal records the journey that I go on as I discover what God has to say on this One Word or theme.

In 2013 I learned how to be *real,* how to have a *real* authentic relationship with God. I discovered what the true *reality* was - God's *reality.*

In 2014, I discovered true *hope* in the most difficult year of my life. I didn't know at the beginning of the year when God chose the word *hope* for me that it was to be my lifeline. I learned that to *hope* was to confidently expect good in my life because of the finished word of Christ. That any situation that comes into my life is not a setback but a step up. I discovered that God uses issues to propel us forward (if we partner with Him) and not to send us backward.

In 2015, *treasure* was my Word or theme. It was enlightening to uncover what my true *treasure* was. Searching for God took on a new meaning as I discovered that He was to be my true *treasure* like the pearl of great price. My journey uncovered what I regard as precious and what was worth *treasuring* up for the future. How the very Spirit of God living inside me was my real *treasure* even though I am but a clay vessel with this precious *treasure* inside. I learned the value of storing up healthy thoughts not toxic ones, storing up health not sickness, storing up finances not debt and storing up *treasure* in heaven by giving to the poor not storing up wealth for ourselves.

Then came the depths of richness in 2016 when I learned to *pause.* This took a lot of discipline and active change. I discovered my voice and the one thing that I was created for. I stopped 'doing' and started 'being'. Priorities were re-evaluated. Goals were set. Silence was embraced. Noise was cancelled. God was listened to. Activities that seemed important were cut. Relationships flourished.

Currently, my One Word is *unleashed.* I am only a quarter of the way through the year but already I have experienced a noticeable shift in my thinking. God is revealing more of Himself and more of my need for Him. I am becoming more aware of my need to be *unleashed* from fears, anxieties, and selfishness. It's like my world has been turned upside down like a salt shaker and God is shaking all the impurities out until the pure stuff is left behind. Becoming *unleashed* in prayer as well as my dream of writing a book resulted in this very book.

Journaling my journey through God's workings is crucial to learning the lessons that I need to go through.

- Gratitude notes -- When I start down the track of feeling sorry for myself and depressing thoughts start to crowd in I get out my journal and start a gratitude list. I list all the things in my life that I am thankful for. This leads to thanking God and praising Him.

- "Aha" moments -- Any revelations from God are noted. Anything that He has made clearer in my mind needs to be recorded so that I can be encouraged later when it is viewed again. I love "aha" moments! They come suddenly, especially while walking or driving. I used to worry that I would forget these "aha" moments and wouldn't be able to record them but now I just pray: *God please help me to remember this so that I can write it down later.* "Aha" moments are like putting in place the last missing piece of a puzzle.

Here is one example: for years I had prayed for clarity in relation to problems. *Please God, show me the way to go. Give me clarity so that I can make the right decision.* Then one day, seemingly out of the blue God speaks (I don't mean a loud voice but through things I read, impressions on my heart or a thought dropped into my mind): *Rachel, you don't need to have clarity in every situation all you need is Christ, my Son, as He is the way, the truth and the life. If you had total clarity there would be no need for a Savior, there would be no need to have faith and trust in Me.*

- Monthly and yearly goals -- In order to keep growing personally and spiritually we need set goals. Not just to set them but to write down action steps in order to achieve our desires.

- Reviews -- I regularly review my journal to *pause* and reread what my journey is like over the month. What has God been teaching me? Where am I growing? What do I need to look at for the next month ahead? How has my One Word or theme been illustrated last month?

- Sermon notes -- Instead of just listening to our pastors preach, why not jot down some notes? It helps to retain what they are teaching and gives you material to review later on. It's putting James 1:22 into action -- to be a doer of the Word and not a hearer only. When I review a portion of my year's journaling I discover God using my Pastors' words to emphasize a lesson that I am learning through my own personal devotions and prayer.

- Prayers -- Requests that I ask from God. As you can see jotting down prayers is only a small part of my journaling but I consider everything that I journal as my two-way conversation with God. Requests are just a small part as I am growing in a relationship not in developing a request checklist to tick off.

- Quotes -- Some people have an amazing ability to write and say succinctly what is on my heart. I just have to write it down!

- Books -- Books I have read or want to read

- Life goals -- It's not just spiritual goals or thoughts but also ideas relating to family, our home, my work, my writing - anything to do with my life. God doesn't work in compartments. He wants to do His work in every area of our lives.

- An Index -- Keeping it practical. I have discovered that my writings become unusable if I quickly look up what I learned on a specific topic. For the past couple of years I have been keeping an index at the back of my journals. Every page in my journal is numbered, and once a month or so I note in the index what the topic is for each page. Now I have an amazing resource of insight into what God has been teaching me and what I have personally grown in.

Take Action

Start your journal today. You don't have to wait until the beginning of the year to do this. Start small. It is something between you and God. Don't try to copy everything I do. This is something that is personal. Everyone's growth is different and I have been keeping journals for nearly 40 years.

Also, don't be legalistic. I can sometimes go for weeks without writing anything in my journal then suddenly have pages and pages filled in one week. Treat it as an organic process, something that is growing with you. It is a tool that is to help you, not something to bring you into bondage.

The goal of journaling is to encourage and keep you in constant communion with God, always looking for growth opportunities. Journaling is the perfect 'abiding in the vine' tool. Start today!

PART THREE:
The Three Prayer Languages Guide

THE PRACTICAL GUIDE TO PRAYING

L et's get down to the nitty gritty - the practical side of praying. **There is a time to stop reading about prayer and just do it.**

The disciples saw how Jesus prayed. It affected them so much that they asked Jesus to teach them to pray. This was the only lesson they had asked of Jesus: "Teach us to pray."[19] They recognized a difference in His prayers. They saw the results of His time alone with the Father and they wanted to be taught by the Master. They saw prayer illustrated by special people dressed in expensive robes entering a holy place. They heard distinguished people standing in the public square lifting their voice loudly in prayer. Prayer to the disciples, didn't seem to be for the ordinary person. Jesus turned their concept of prayer upside down. What He shared was surprising. It wasn't a long formula with big fancy words but a simple template for the ordinary person.

So Where Is a Good Place to Pray?

Jesus said "But when you pray, go into your most private room, close the door and pray to your Father who is in secret" (Matthew 6:6 AMP).

This 'private room' is the Greek word *tameion* which was really a store room.[20] The King James Version calls it a *closet*. It probably was the only room in the house and was used to store tools and other items. It was not a place that you would invite your guests to see. It was private. In today's world it would be a garage, smelly, dirty and full of everyday equipment. A far cry from a sacred holy place in a temple. But this is where we are to meet with our Heavenly Father according to Jesus.

I love that Jesus gave us an example of where to pray. We don't have to have a special room set aside, our war-room. No need for a special prayer chair with a basket full of journals and pretty pens. No, just an everyday messy place is perfect for meeting with the God of the universe. As soon as we say "Our Father in heaven" we are standing on holy ground.

It doesn't matter where you pray -- in a church, in your car, walking the dog, in the shower, in your bed. Everywhere and anywhere is included.

"Where can I go from Your Spirit?
Or where can I flee from Your presence?
If I ascend to heaven, You are there;
If I make my bed in Sheol, behold You are there.
If I take the wings of the dawn,
If I dwell in the remotest part of the sea,
Even there Your hand will lead me,
And Your right hand will lay hold of me.
(Psalm 139:7-10 NASB)

Jesus wanted His disciples to know that ordinary people can pray in their ordinary homes. That's great news! We all matter to God. He desires to talk with each one of His children in whatever circumstance we find ourselves in. We don't need to wait until the time is right. We don't have to wait until Sunday morning in church to pray. Don't wait until you have a *closet* to pray. Pray right where you are. In your pyjamas. Or on your way to work. Standing on the soccer field. **The everyday place is holy ground when we pray.**

"Prayer is not a privilege for the pious, not the art of a chosen few. Prayer is simply a heartfelt conversation between God and his child."[21]

Who Are We Praying To?

For centuries, the people of God prayed to the great I AM. The Creator of the heaven and earth, El Shaddai, God Almighty, the God on the fiery mountain that no one but Moses wanted to approach. All of this is true but God also wanted to be called upon as a Father.

"When Israel was a child, I loved him, and out of Egypt I called my son." (Hosea 11:1).

The people had forgotten God as Father when Jesus was walking the earth. In Jesus' little lesson on prayer he cuts straight to the Who we are talking to: "Our Father which art in heaven, hallowed be thy name." (Matthew 6:9 KJV).

We are talking to our Heavenly Father when we pray. Whatever type of earthly father you had, he won't come close to what your Father in heaven is like. Your Heavenly Father is perfect. He knows what you need and who you are. No pretending needed. No introductions required. He knows what you are all about. He completely understands you. In fact He knows what you are going to say to Him before you even say it, but He still wants to hear it. Like all good dads, He doesn't want you to be concerned about anything. He wants to take care of it all.

"Give all your worries and cares to God, for he cares for you." (1 Peter 5:7 NLT).

When I am in 'asking prayer' mode, I picture myself as a little girl running into my daddy's throne room and calling out, *Daddy please help me, I have a problem.* We are not praying to a faraway entity that is ready to hit us over the knuckles if we mess up. We are not praying to a statue made by man. We are not praying to a past ancestor. No, we are praying to our Father who, through Jesus, has adopted us as his child. He knows us intimately more than we even know ourselves.

"You made all the delicate, inner parts of my body and knit me together in my mother's womb." (Psalm 139:13 NLT).

If you have difficulty with prayer it would be a good idea to dwell on the Who of prayer. Think about the most caring attentive earthly father that you know, multiply that by infinity and that's God, our heavenly Father. Knowing this should make a difference in our prayer life.

When Are We to Pray?

"Be constant in prayer." (Romans 12:12b).

I consider prayer to have no time limit. I am not going to tell you to wake up at 5:30 am to spend an hour in prayer with God. Prayer is not something that we do to tick off a list. Tick, did my fifteen minute devotion. Tick, did my prayer hour. No, prayer is a lifestyle.

Creating a life that has a flow of conversation between you and God is the key. It is the only way to follow what Paul wrote in Romans chapter 12, to be constant in prayer. The Greek word for constant is *proskartereo* which means to be devoted to. To give unremitting care to a thing. To persevere and not faint.[22] It is the idea of something stuck to something else, completely devoted, no pulling away.

As a teenager and young adult, I was always fearful that I wasn't doing enough for God. I remember listening to many sermons that exhorted me to spend an hour in prayer daily. If I wasn't doing that then I must be a weak Christian. Being a very conscientious person, I came under such guilt when I didn't achieve this standard.

I broke free from the slavery to prayer rules when I realized that prayer is about creating a daily rhythm of conversation with your heavenly Father. Now that I have made this realization God is part of my day. When I awake, I say *Good morning, God*. I chat to Him about the day ahead. The main conversation is held when I walk. Walk and talk. We talk about the projects that I have. I bring him my concerns for my sons and husband. I ask Him for His help. I pass over my worries. I then pass over worries that I have already passed over, still working on that. I thank Him. I praise Him. I listen. During the day, I shoot quick prayers to Him. *Help Father, I don't know what to say to this person, Please help me to find the answer here.* At the end of the day, I fall asleep talking to Him. **A daily rhythm of talking and listening to God with no time limits brings freedom.**

How to Pray?

Keeping it simple is the best. Jesus gave us a pattern in what is called The Lord's Prayer. I love how Max Lucado, in his book <u>Before Amen: The Power of a Simple Prayer</u>, sets it out:

"It seems to me that the prayers of the Bible can be distilled into one. The result is a simple, easy to remember, pocket-size prayer:

> Father
> You are good.
> I need help. Heal me & forgive me.
> They need help.
> Thank you.
> In Jesus Name Amen.

Let this prayer punctuate your day."[23]

This prayer is real. It's down to earth. No fancy talk. Straight to the point. We don't need to give God a run down on the back story to our prayer. He knows it already. He's your Dad and He was there before you were born.

Here Is My Simple Take on Jesus' Pattern:

> Dad, please help
> Thanks Dad, I love you
> Dad, what do you think?

Just three simple elements to a praying lifestyle. Another way of stating the pattern:

Petition

Praise

Praying the Word

All three elements are needed. All three are what God desires. God wants us to call on Him for help and to ask Him for our daily bread. Praising and thanking God is incredibly powerful and not to be left out. Praying the Word is simply reminding God of His very own Words. It's taking up the sword of the Spirit as a weapon as described by Paul in the letter to the Ephesians.

Take Action

Prayer is not just for preachers and missionaries but necessary for everyday ordinary people. It is supposed to be as simple as breathing. It's the communication of a loving relationship between a person and her heavenly Dad. As we prepare to go deeper into each one of these three elements based on Jesus' pattern think about your current prayer life. Are you favoring one above the other? Do all three elements appear in some way? All three are powerful and essential to our Christian walk and growth.

ASK: Dad, Please Help

Petition prayer, asking God for help, is probably the most common way of communicating. But it can also be put aside. I have found this in my own life. That guilty feeling that I can't be asking God for stuff all the time. So, we try to do life independently until we really get into a jam. The thing is God wants us, no, He desires us to ask Him. Jesus told us to ask for our daily bread from our heavenly Father. That is getting down to the basics. God is interested in us asking for the basics of life.

God has given us some impressive promises. Here are three that come from the mouth of Jesus Himself that just blows my socks off:

Impressive Promise 1

"And whatever you ask in prayer, you will receive, if you have faith." (Matthew 21:22). In the Message Bible it says "Absolutely everything, ranging from small to large, as you make it part of your believing prayer, gets included as you lay hold of God."

Impressive Promise 2

"Ask, and it will be given to you; seek, and you will find; knock, and it will be opened to you." (Matthew 7:7).

Impressive Promise 3

"If you remain in me and my words remain in you, ask whatever you want, and it will be done for you." (John 15:7).

These are pretty amazing promises. The word 'whatever' seems to appear a number of times. In essence, without asking we don't receive. Even James says, "Yet you don't have what you want because you don't ask God for it." (James 4:2b NLT).

What is the Main Purpose of Asking?

Why ask? I believe that God wants us to live worry free. He wants us to ask Him daily for our physical, mental, emotional and financial needs. All good fathers want to provide for their children's needs and wants. All good fathers want the best for their kids. The best education, friends, opportunities, mentors, life partner and the best character. It's the same with our Heavenly Father. He wants us to have His best plan. Of course, frequently His best plan and our idea of what is best doesn't always match.

My main goal in praying is to develop a deep meaningful relationship with the Lord. I also want to see God turn up in my everyday life. I want to see His fingerprints on the moments of my day. God wants to turn up in our days but it does involve us asking Him to.

What Can We Ask For?

I want to seek the extraordinary in my life. I don't want to just survive, I want to thrive as a believer. To thrive and grow in prayer we need to broaden the limits of our petition prayers. Here are five categories of petition prayers that you can actively grow in and see God turn up in your days:

- People Prayers
- Personal Growth Prayers
- Physical Needs Prayers

- Planet Prayers
- Problem Prayers

Some are ordinary: praying for our problems and physical needs, but others are not as common: praying for random people that come across your path. Even with the ordinary praying for our problems, there is always room for growth. Giving all of our problems to God is challenging, and I am not there yet on that one. It is a constant battle for me to cast those worries over to Him, but it is one worth fighting.

People Prayers

People are a major part of our lives aren't they? We are part of families, schools, work places, churches and neighborhoods. People are everywhere. John Doone, the English philosopher said, "No man is an island."[24]

God realized when He created Adam that it was not good for Adam to be alone; he needed a companion. Whether we are an extrovert or introvert we need to get along with people. Because people are so involved in our personal world we will find ourselves talking to God about them or maybe complaining to God about them. Sometimes it is hard to know how to pray for the people in our lives. Here are a few ideas to help when you are unsure how to pray.

Praying for Your Partner and Your Marriage

I am going to share with you one prayer based on a scripture verse that has revolutionized my marriage. When you have been married to someone for a long time (we are coming up to twenty five years married) you get comfortable, don't you? The romance dies off and the daily grind takes over. Seasons tick over and it is easy to drift slowly apart. I didn't want that to happen.

I want a marriage that is constantly improving, getting better and better over time. I desire our love to deepen every day. I asked God for His take on this because I always want to pray His plans. He led me to Colossians 2:2 and this has been my prayer for the past five to ten years. It was a prayer that Paul had for the believers at Laodicea. One phrase hit me and has been my long term prayer for my marriage.

"[For my hope is] that their hearts may be encouraged as they are *knit together in [unselfish] love*, so that they may have all the riches that come from the full assurance of understanding [the joy of salvation] resulting in a true [and more intimate]

knowledge of the mystery of God, that is Christ."
(Colossians 2:2 AMP, *emphasis mine*)

That is my hope, my desire for our marriage that we live with hearts that are encouraged not discouraged as two hearts that are strong. Hearts that are encouraged are strong. How are these two hearts to be built up, improving and getting better and stronger over time? By *being knitted together in love*. The Message version says, "I want you woven into a tapestry of love, in touch with everything there is to know of God. Then you will have minds confident and at rest, focused on Christ, God's great mystery."

I pray it as a general prayer whenever I pray about our marriage but also as a specific prayer in the middle of a disagreement or if we are irritated with each other. I pray, *God, please help us to know your truth in this situation. Please show me any selfish way in me. Please continue to knit me together in love with my husband.* This prayer is so powerful! It changes feelings, it highlights what is important and it heals brokenness. Since praying God's words into our marriage I see a strength developing and a love deepening with each passing year.

Praying for Your Friends

There was a rich guy named Job who fell on rough times. He lost his home, his children, his business and his health. He was in dire circumstances. This guy, Job was a believer in God, a strong believer. He had a couple of friends who were trying to help but were more discouraging than uplifting. Of course I am talking about Job from the pages of the Bible. God blessed him in the end with double what he had lost, but do you know what preceded this blessing from God?

"When Job prayed for his friends, the Lord restored his fortunes. In fact, the Lord gave him twice as much as before!" (Job 42:10 NLT).

What came first was prayer. Job prayed for his friends. The very guys that were not helping at all, but were depressing to listen to. His friends spoke things of God that were not right. They kept on telling him that the cause of his problems was his own sin. God was angry against these guys. Job took the time and energy out to bring his friends before God and pray for them. This was no small feat, and by praying for his friends, Job was essentially forgiving them. The next thing that happens in Job's life is restoration and blessing.

There is a strong connection here between prayer for people, forgiveness and restoration in your own life. Maybe it has something to do with taking your focus off your own problems and placing it on other people. But for Job, a big part, the act of praying for his friends, was also the act of letting go of any resentment towards them. He wanted them restored to God as well as himself.

There are many verses in the Bible that talk about praying for each other. Here are just two:

"Confess your sins to each other and pray for each other so that you may be healed. The earnest prayer of a righteous person has great power and produces wonderful results." (James 5:16 NLT).

"Pray in the Spirit at all times and on every occasion. Stay alert and be persistent in your prayers for all believers everywhere." (Ephesians 6:18 NLT).

Did you catch the benefits of praying for each other? Healing. The Greek word used here means *to heal, to cure, to make whole.* There are so many parts of a person life that need curing and wholeness. Not just physically but mentally and emotionally. What brings about this healing? Earnest, persistent and constant prayer.

Sometimes it feels like nothing is happening and it is so easy to give up praying for your friends. But James gives us hope that our prayers have the ability to be powerful and produce wonderful results! Keep going. Don't give up now; the breakthrough may just be around the corner.

Praying for Your Enemies

Okay, so this one is hard. Praying for your enemies is a challenge. People who are your enemies are usually not on a friendly basis with you. Jesus had some hard words to swallow in regard to praying for your enemies:

"You have heard that it was said, 'you shall love your neighbor and hate your enemy.' But I say to you, love your enemies and pray for those who persecute you, so that you may be sons of your Father who is in heaven." (Matthew 5:43-45).

Praying for your enemies is a sign that you are truly a child of God. It signifies that you have a heart after God's heart. His heart is for everyone to come to know the truth. His heart is to see people come into relationship with Him. It is not easy to pray for people who have hurt you in the past or continue to hurt you. But God requires it of us. If we choose not to pray for our enemies we are really hurting ourselves.

So, who are our enemies? Is it people who hurt us personally? Yes. But I think Jesus was also talking about the global picture: enemies to the cross. He wants us to pray for Islamic extremists and dictators who are against Christianity. Pray for their salvation. There have been many stories of Muslims coming face to face with Jesus and repenting. Pray that the evil that they want to inflict won't happen, that it is restrained.

Personal Growth Prayers

The Self Improvement industry is huge. All generations seem to be interested in improving themselves, from diet plans and exercise workouts to life coaching and counseling. In one survey 84% of the Baby Boomer's Generation admitted to spending an average of $152 a month on self-improvement while 94% of Millennials on average spent over $300 per month.[25]

I am definitely a goal and task oriented person. I love having a plan and sticking to it. My training as a Chartered Accountant is geared to personal development, continuous learning and increasing efficiencies. So you can imagine that I am drawn to the self-improvement industry. I don't want to stay the same. I want each year to be an improvement on the last. I know as a Believer I have to be careful that my goals and plans are God's idea as well. My focus needs to be Christ-centered and not self-centered. Our motives and intentions are what God looks at. He judges the heart.

"But the Lord said to Samuel, "Do not look on his appearance or on the height of his stature, because I have rejected him. For the Lord sees not as man sees: man looks on the outward appearance, but the Lord looks on the heart." (1 Samuel 16:7).

When we ask our Heavenly Father for help are we asking for God to be glorified or are we seeking our own glory? Sometimes it is subtle and it is easy to deceive ourselves.

"And even when you ask, you don't get it because your motives are all wrong--you want only what will give you pleasure." (James 4:3 NLT).

I find myself frequently praying for a comfortable life. I think we all do, don't we? It's only natural to ask for comfort. But is it God's idea? Yes, God wants us to live worry free in peace, but that doesn't mean that all our issues just disappear. It does mean that His peace is on tap, that He will never leave us nor forsake us. We have everything we need to live this life through Jesus.

"By his divine power, God has given us everything we need for living a godly life. We have received all of this by coming to know Him, the one who called us to Himself by means of His marvelous glory and excellence." (2 Peter 1:3 NLT).

We have everything we need to endure all things. In the love chapter of 1 Corinthians (chapter 13) it tells us that love endures all things. God is love, and we have His Spirit living in us. This enables us to endure all things.

God is interested in our personal development. He desires growth in us. Jesus chose us for a reason: to bear fruit. "You did not choose me, but I chose you and appointed you that you should go and bear fruit." (John 15:16). But as we work on our own development, whether it be losing weight, becoming positive thinkers or developing our life plan, we need to have Christ as the center of it all.

Set Godly Goals

We pray. We commit our plans into His hands for Him to advance, or say wait or stop. "Commit your works to the Lord and your plans will be established." (Proverbs 16:3).

This is the first step to any life plan or goal list. Pray. Tell God the actions you would like to take in the next 30 or 90 days. Ask Him to reveal His plans to you. Ask for guidance and wisdom. Seek His truth, and ask if there are any plans that are not good for you to undertake be made clear.

Keep your goals flexible. Why? *God seems to release information on a need to know basis.* That is why faith and trust is crucial in our Christian walk. I have discovered that it is good to pray and set goals, but also to be willing to change direction as soon as God leads. I can't do that if my goals and plans are rigid. This usually happens if I am not willing to keep a listening ear to God.

What If You Don't Know What Your Goals Are?

Knowing your goals isn't always easy. How can you commit to God what you are unsure of? I believe strongly that God wants you to have goals. He has actions He wants you to take this year. He has specific plans that require your personality and unique abilities. He desires to let you know what these plans are. He may not reveal the whole plan, but at least the first step. Believe this. Pray for this.

If this is your position right now then this is your first step.

God might be wanting to do a 'new thing' in your life. "Behold the former things have come to pass, and new things I declare; before they spring forth I tell you of them." (Isaiah 42:9). What a great promise! God may have new things to declare over your life. He promises to let you know what they are before they arrive. Take that word and pray: *Father, thank you for the new things that you have for me. Thank you for your promise to let me know before they arrive.*

Praying for God's Ideas

God is the creator of everything we see and don't see. He is the One that has placed wonderful, creative ideas into people. The writer of the book of Hebrews tells us in chapter twelve that we are to look to Jesus who is the author and finisher of our faith. Our personal development program, whether it is a spiritual, physical or work related program, involves faith in God. It involves seeking God to start and trusting that God will help you to finish the course.

As a home-school mom this truth has freed me from trying to develop our home-school program on my own. I can pray: God you started this amazing home-school journey and I trust that you will help me bring it to completion now that my sons have grown. I thank you for past ideas and pray for fresh new ones straight from heaven. You know my sons and what they need from me for their education. I ask for your ideas to fill my mind and help me to develop them into a program for this year.

God wants to give you His ideas to help you in your life. In Jeremiah 33:3 He says, "Call to me and I will answer you, and will tell you great and hidden things that you have not known." God is saying that He wants to tell us new things that we didn't know before. New things, new knowledge and ideas that will help us. New ideas for getting that weight off once and for all. New ideas on how to parent that difficult child. New ideas on how to speak to people if you are shy. New ideas on how to do better at work or school. New ideas on how to save money.

There have been many instances of God giving people ideas in their dreams that have changed the world. Dmitri Mendeleev had spent months trying to work out how to logically organize the chemical elements. He said, "In a dream I saw a table where all the elements fell into place as required. Awakening, I immediately wrote it down on a piece of paper."[26] Einstein's theory of relativity was inspired by a dream as well.

Proverbs 8:12 calls God's ideas as witty inventions. "I, wisdom dwell with prudence, and find out knowledge of witty inventions." (Proverbs 8:12 KJV). If we are asking God in prayer for wisdom for our plans we are also asking Him for His ideas, for His witty inventions. These are things that we don't know. How can we pray for something that we don't know? By praying the Word.

Father, I need help. I need your wisdom to go forward in my life. You say in your word for me to call on you so I am calling on you now. Thank you that you will answer me. I ask that you will tell me great and hidden things - God ideas - that I don't know now. Widen my reality to your reality. Show me what you see in this situation. Uncover my eyes to the solution or the best way forward. Help me plan my year, this week and today with your wisdom. Praise you Father.

Praying for God's Wisdom

You may already have ideas but you just are not sure how to go about bringing the ideas into action. You need God's wisdom. He knows all things. He knows the future. He is our best source of wisdom. "The Lord by wisdom founded the earth. By understanding He established the heavens. By His knowledge the deeps were broken up and the skies drip with dew." (Proverbs 3:19-20). Think on that. The earth was founded on the wisdom of God. Scientists today are still discovering the makeup of the earth. We have direct access to the same wisdom that founded this earth.

In the book of Exodus it talks about how the sanctuary was constructed. God chose certain men to be artists and builders of His meeting place with man. In chapter 35 it tells us that God filled these men with the spirit of God, in wisdom, in understanding and in knowledge and in all manner of workmanship.[27] Let's pray for that same dose of God's wisdom, understanding and knowledge to fill us and our children so that we may do good work.

There is a phrase that is repeated throughout Proverbs and other parts of the Hebrew Scriptures: *the fear of the Lord is the beginning of wisdom.*[28]

Before we can have wisdom we need the fear of the Lord. I think that we show that we fear God when we defer to Him first in all things. Before you next project, at the beginning of setting your goals, as you plan your finances, turn to God and ask for His wisdom in your preparations and goal setting. I believe that He wants us to be using our time well. Let's not waste time on trying to accomplish tasks on our own. Let's pray for His wisdom and for the best way to accomplish the goals that He has laid on our heart.

Praying Through Your Priorities

I have come to realize that understanding what my priorities are is crucial to moving forward and achieving goals. Priorities are those things that you regard, deep down, as most important in your life. I have discovered that sometimes I am in denial over my true priorities.

Take weight loss. For years I have had a priority to lose weight, or so I thought. If I really did have a weight loss priority I would have lost weight, right? It sounds simple but it is so easy to delude ourselves into thinking that we have right priorities when we are really sabotaging ourselves instead. I also thought that God was my number one priority, that my relationship with Him was the most important above everything else. But when I sat down and really counted my time, feelings, thoughts and actions I discovered the opposite. I was spending more time watching TV than reading God's word or talking with Him in prayer. Most of my days were spent serving my own interests and not God's. There was no walking by the Spirit happening. I think most of us are in the same boat if we were all honest with ourselves.

If we want to grow personally, whether that be spiritually, relationally, financially or emotionally, we need to take a deep review of our priorities. What you find might shock you. I know that I was shocked when I woke up to the facts that my health and God were at the bottom of my list. Family and work was at the top. It was all upside down. I needed God and my health to move up to the top spot. It is no use having godly goals like growing spiritually, losing weight or saving money and having conflicting priorities. You are not going to achieve your goals this way. Your priorities and your goals need to match, not conflict.

To make these changes prayer is needed so that God can open up your eyes to see the truth of your life. He can show you what your true priorities are. It takes courage to face up to the truth. To take your head out of the sand and see where your life is heading. Don't be discouraged by what God shows you. Just be thankful that you now know the truth; Jesus says that knowing truth sets you free.[29] You are now free to move forward towards your goals.

Look over your goals. Think about what you want to see happen in your life for this year. Write down what things need to be of high priority for your goals to be achieved. If you want to lose weight then health needs to be a top priority. If health was a priority then taking a daily walk or some form of exercise would feature in your calendar, right? If it is a priority then you incorporate a habit of daily exercise without fail. If your health is extremely important to you then you would find the best eating plan for your body. You would spend as much time as you are able in making sure that you are consuming the right food in the appropriate portion sizes, right?

If your goal is to save a certain amount of money for a project or to pay off debt, you would make the time to set a budget, monitor your spending, and set up a savings account. Maybe you would have saving or debt reduction weekly or monthly targets, and every purchase would be reviewed against your priority to save.

A shift is required to move you from your current priority list to your desired priority list. I am becoming more convinced that any personal change only occurs when a person has shifted her priorities. What if you desire different priorities to match your goals but you find yourself not following through? Your body seems to have a different set of priorities that it is following. I hear you. This is where the battle is. Take heart; you are nearly there. Discovering that you are operating on the wrong priorities for your goals is the first and biggest step. You are now out in the open -- truth territory. It only gets better from here. Now it is time to make a quality decision.

This decision is important. Your heart and mind is telling the rest of you that change is happening. This change is for the better. It is going to be painful as the change happens but the end result is going to be worth it. This is where you tell yourself that you are committed to the new priorities, that they are the new you. You tell yourself that you will do whatever it takes to stick to those new priorities. A shift in what you value needs to occur. Instead of valuing comfort by eating comfort food and not moving you are going to value health by eating good quality fuel and moving your body. Instead of valuing convenience and instant gratification you are going to value delayed gratification and making your money work for you.

This is a big step which is probably missed out by most people. If there isn't a value and priority shift then setting goals will not change anything in your life. It is really bringing your whole spirit, soul and body into line so all of you is moving in the same direction. **Talking to God about this priority shift is valuable. He knows all about you. He can help you to make the shift. He wants you to grow and mature in all areas of your life.**

"Beloved, I pray that in every way you may succeed and prosper and be in good health [physically], just as [I know] your soul prospers [spiritually]." (3 John 1:2 AMP). We can see from this prayer of Peter's that God wishes you to succeed and prosper physically and spiritually. This is good news!

Write Down Your Vision

After time in prayer, thinking and in the Word you should have some idea of what your goals are for the coming year, or at least the next step. These goals or plans need to be written down. There is something powerful that happens when pen connects with paper and our ideas and plans are written down. Something tangible is now created. Thoughts and ideas become a written statement of intent.

"And the Lord answered me: 'write the vision; make it plain on tablets, so he may run who reads it.'" (Habakkuk 2:2).

This written vision is used as a reminder of what you are aiming for as well as a prayer reminder. I have visualized my list of goals and printed and pasted it into my journal and also posted them on the bathroom wall where it is seen frequently.

According to research conducted by Dr. Gail Matthews, a psychology professor at Dominican University in California, you are 42 percent more likely to achieve your goals by writing them down.[30] God knew that. He made us to be visual people. He made us to declare the end from the beginning. Thinking about your goals takes place in your right hemisphere of your brain but when you take it a step further and write down your goals you are tapping into the power of your left hemisphere, the logic side. This sends a signal to the cells in your body that you really, really want this![31] Now, imagine the increased likelihood of achieving your goals when you have already prayed at their inception, having written them down and continuing to pray them into existence while you are physically working on them. Powerful stuff.

Pray for Mentors

I don't believe that God wants us to do life on our own. His plan for his children is a community of people sharing their lives together. His desire is to see us mentoring each other, being mentored and mentoring others.

What is a mentor? According to the dictionary.com it is a wise and trusted counselor or teacher- an influential senior supporter.[32] A mentor is basically a guide, someone who has gone before us, someone who can inspire us towards personal and spiritual growth, an encourager.

Proverbs 27:17 describes mentoring as iron sharpening iron. That is exactly what happens when you spend time with someone who is further along life's journey from you. Your rough edges are smoothed away. Your purpose and focus becomes more defined and clear. Light is turned on and you can clearly see your life path ahead of you. Mentoring is the modern term for making disciples. In our pursuit of personal and spiritual growth, having a mentor is valuable and can shorten the time it takes to learn and grow. They can give you encouragement - they have been where you are and can offer advice from past experiences. They can help you form your vision, discover your passion and purpose plus set out the steps to get there. A mentor can provide accountability. This component is vital. Having someone who can check up regularly on how you are progressing towards your goals will keep you on the path to success.

How do you find such a person? Pray for one! Father God, I thank you for your church. That there are other Believers on the earth that have faced the same situations as me. Thank you Lord that you have a plan for my life with a purpose and vision. Thank you for showing me what that is. I pray and ask now that you will provide a mentor for me. Someone to encourage, inspire and challenge me. Help me to recognize who you have selected. Help me to benefit from their mentoring. Help me to give back to others just as I have received. Thank you Jesus. I ask in your name, Amen.

Keep your eyes open. Your mentor may not be who you think God will bring along. God could bring a book into your life where the author's life and words resonate with you. This author could be your mentor for right now. If this is the case, check out the author's website or blog. Read other books written by her. Google to see if she has done any podcasts and listen to them while out walking or driving. There is a lot of sound spiritual mentoring support readily available on the Internet and in books. Ask God to point you in the right direction.

If God does bring a person into your life it is usually for a season. Maybe even one point of time in the form of a conversation or an email. Sometimes this may be over a year or two. We are all at different levels and seasons, and God, in His infinite wisdom, knows this. He provides the right instruction and people at the right times. Appreciate these times and people. Don't suck everything out of them or monopolize their time. And always be respectful.

What if you just seem to be doing life on your own? No mentors. No inspiration. Nothing. There is good news. Every believer has The Ultimate Mentor. This mentor never leaves us -- ever. He is always around. He never gets tired of our questions or mess-ups. He has always got the right advice and encouragement. I am talking about the Holy Spirit who resides in each believer.

Jesus, while talking with his disciples, said, "But the Helper, the Holy Spirit, whom the Father will send in my name, he will teach you all things and bring to your remembrance all that I have said to you." (John

14:26). God's very Spirit is the Ultimate Mentor. Human mentors get tired, they can let us down. But God's Spirit never lets us down. The Holy Spirit needs to be your number one, go-to mentor before everyone and everything else. The more you value the Holy Spirit's input into your life the more you will hear from Him. There will be times in your life where you are all alone, and there is not a human being who can fully understand your situation or give you good advice or encouragement. Only the Holy Spirit can be the one to comfort and teach you. He is the amazing gift that was promised so long ago, and we are the fortunate generation that gets to experience His mentoring.

It helps your personal and spiritual growth to also give back and mentor others. God knows just the right people who need what you have. People who are behind you on the path and need to know what you know from your experience. There are people who could gain from what you have learned. Be open to being utilized by God to be their mentor. Pray to be mentored and to mentor others. You will be blessed and be a blessing to others.

Setting Action Steps Prayerfully

So, you have your godly goals sorted; you've prayed for God's ideas. You have some of vision or overall big plan. You have written this all down. You have prayed for a mentor. What next? How do you get from setting goals to achieving them?

It is common for a believer to include God in their vision and big goal planning, but when it comes to the nitty gritty they seem to leave God out and prayer stops. God wants to be included in everything, from the inception of an idea through to completion and everything in between. The big in-between is where we need God the most! It is easy to get off track, forget the initial reason behind the idea or plan and start going down a road that God never desired you to go down. But it doesn't have to be that way.

Here is a great verse to believe and put into action: "If you then, who are evil, know how to give good gifts to your children, how much more will your Father who is in heaven give good things to those who ask him!" (Matthew 7:11). Do we really believe this? God as our Father wants us to personally grow here in our earthly lives and spiritually. He is interested in our goals, visions and plans. He is interested in our personal development journey. He doesn't want us to stay the same as we were ten years ago or even one year ago.

Paul, in his second letter to the Corinthians, tells us that "we are to be transformed into the image of the glory of the Lord from one degree of glory to another." (2 Corinthians 3:18). In order to do that, we need action steps as part of our plan. Sometimes we don't know what these action steps should be and we need to pray for God's wisdom and His action steps. God, as our Father, loves to hear His kids asking for action steps. He wants to give us good gifts as Jesus tells us in Matthew 7:11. Action steps that move us closer to our goals are good gifts. Pray and ask God for His action steps.

Prayerful Regular Reviews

Michael Hyatt says in his book <u>Living Forward: A Proven Plan to Stop Drifting and Get the Life you Want</u>, "A plan is worthless unless you review it on a regular basis."[33] He talks about having "a process in place for making" your plan visible. This is where regular reviews come in to play. If we don't regularly review our goals and action steps we will have no idea whether we are achieving what we set out to do or whether we need to tweak our action steps in order to stay on the journey.

Set up review times according to the timing of your action steps. For example, if you have a weekly target for weight loss you may want to have a weekly review session to write down your weight and review your week's exercise and eating habits that contributed to the resulting gain or loss. While I was losing weight my reviews were weekly; I wanted to keep a tight grip on what was happening. Now, most of my goals are on a monthly basis. This includes things like the number of words I am writing or general personal development goals. I sit down once a month and write a page in my journal on what I have achieved in the past month and what God has taught me. I review my goals and plans, reminding myself of what is important. I might have verses that God has given me for my vision and goals and I repeat these, maybe even writing them out again. Then I take a page to write my goals for the coming month. These answer questions such as: What activities do I have that I need to prepare for? What targets do I need to meet in order to move closer to achieving my big goal for the year? Do I need to set some weekly goals to achieve the monthly targets?

These regular reviews need to include God. When we pray at the beginning for His ideas and His vision we should also pray for His action steps and help. We also need to lay our time and actions before Him and review our progress with Him. He can show us what has improved and what needs more work. He can open our eyes to issues that we can't comprehend or don't want to face. He can show us the truth, and knowing the full truth can set us free to accomplish those goals.

Prayerfully reviewing your goals and where you are at is vital to moving forward in your life. Don't be one of the masses who sets goals and then forget them. Be the person who is determined to keep moving forward in their life. To move from one level of glory to another. To personally and spiritually develop and grow. Growth involves regularly reviewing where we are and what it will take to get where we want to go.

God is interested in your personal and spiritual growth. He wants you to talk with Him on every facet of your life.

Physical Needs Prayers

Jesus teaches us in Matthew 6:11 to ask God to "give us today the food we need". God desires for us to ask Him for our physical needs. Paul tells us in Philippians "And this same God who takes care of me will supply all your needs from His glorious riches, which have been given to us in Christ Jesus" (Philippians 4:19 NLT). I would like to share how God has taught me to pray for two physical needs: shelter and health.

Praying for a Home

Owning our own home is one of the longest, biggest request I have prayed. I know many families who have a desire to stop renting and live in their own home. It was my deep desire for 13 years to stop renting and save for deposit for our own home, a constant prayer request. I needed to keep believing that God's timing is perfect, although, I found it hard to wait.

Where I live, in New Zealand, it is extremely expensive to rent and we are strongly encouraged and expected to save for a deposit to buy our own home, then have a family and pay off the mortgage by the time you are in your forties. New Zealand has only recently implemented a retirement savings scheme for workers so the main source of retirement savings is a debt free home. Well, we haven't been the typical Kiwi family. We have owned our own business for 10 years while the boys were young. This was a struggle and left nothing over to save for a home. We also home-schooled our sons from the time they were little until they went to tertiary study, most of this time as a one income family. That doesn't help towards owning our own home. I wouldn't want to change our decision to home-school or to have our own property maintenance business. The benefits far outweighed the costs. But it did mean that we were still renting in our mid-forties.

There were times when I tried to "help" God out and took things into my own hands. That never seemed to work. Most of the time I had to just wait and pray while being wise with our finances. I had a deep conviction that God called me to home-school my sons and that came first, before a home.

God is in the restoration business especially when it comes to His children. I held onto a promise He gave me near the end of my 13 year wait in Joel 2:25 "I will restore to you the years that the swarming locust has eaten." All those years of educating my sons on one income while paying rent into someone else's pocket, God had promised to restore. The word restore is the Hebrew word *shalam* which comes from the word *shalom* meaning peace. *Shalam* means to be complete, to make good, to make whole. [34]

God led us through some severe difficulties over a period of 18 months before the restoration started. We lost a main client in our business which led to the decision to close the company down and move to Australia for work in the mining industry. We sold most of our possessions and temporarily moved the family in with my parents while my husband went to Australia to work. Then a serious car accident happened. Our entire savings disappeared to pay for the accident and living expenses while waiting for the first work contract. Homeless. Jobless. But not faithless. God had not given up on us and I had not given up on God. I clung to hope. I clung to a verse in Romans: "And we know that all things work together for good for those who love God, who are called according to his purpose." (Romans 8:28 NET). I clung to Psalm 23 praying: "God is our shepherd - we shall not want." (Psalm 23:1).

Things were going to get tougher still. I ended up in bed with a back injury. Then my husband's new contract was terminated the first day that he arrived on the site. The company had gone into liquidation; over 1,200 men had lost their jobs and were sent back to Perth, Australia. We just had enough money to buy him a ticket home. What were we going to do now? Things looked hopeless. How could we buy our own home when we had no security and no jobs? Had God forgotten about us? When was this restoration going to take place?

God is always faithful. He always keeps His word. It says in Psalm 84:11 that the Lord withholds no good thing from those that walk uprightly. A place to live, shelter, is a good thing. I reminded the Lord in prayer, *God, you say in Your word that You withhold no good thing. Shelter for my family is a good thing, jobs are a good thing. So I pray that you release these good things into our hands.* God was reminding me at this time, that He can do the impossible. I would be reading in the Word about

Joseph seeing that one moment he was in prison and then the next day he was 2nd in charge of Egypt. I held onto that. I labeled that year the "Year of Hope." A couple of months later we both received good job offers; praise God! About this time I felt an impression from God to get ready for our new home. We were still living with my parents, two of our sons still sleeping in the garage, but we had jobs. I got the impression that the house would happen quickly. I had assumed quick meant I would need to be prepared to make quick decisions on wallpaper and paint colors. But quick meant that I had to know what a good buy was. I had been researching open homes on trademe.com which made me depressed. How could we afford these homes?

Through a series of events in one week, we saw our home for twenty minutes at night the day before the auction, and miracle of miracles, we were the successful bidders at the auction. It was a house that had been seized by the government in a fraud case. Now it was time for the owner to repay the bank and leave the country. Years previous, I had written down the details that I would want and need in a home in my journal. Number of bedrooms, study, garage, and family room. I wanted a roomy family home for loads of teenagers. This home ticked every single prayer request and more. It's not perfect. We have a long list of repairs and renovations that need to be done but it is ours. The amazing thing is when I looked back through my journal the exact month that I prayed and asked God for the specific details of our own home was the exact month that the government had seized the home five years before we had won it at auction. God is so good. He had planned that we would receive this house.

If you have been waiting and praying for a house don't give up. Keep praying. Keep believing. God withholds no good thing from those who walk uprightly. I encourage you to seek God for your home. Ask Him for scriptures that you can place your hope on.

Praying for Health

God, as our Heavenly Father, wants us to be well and in health. Jesus taught in Matthew 7:11 "If you then, who are evil, know how to give good gifts to your children, how much more will your Father who is in heaven give good things to those who ask him!" All good fathers want their children to be healthy and healed from sickness and disease. God calls himself Jehovah Rapha, the God who heals, in Exodus 15:26.

The main portion of Jesus' ministry on earth was healing people. "Jesus traveled throughout the region of Galilee, teaching in the synagogues and announcing the Good News about the Kingdom. And he healed every kind of disease and illness. News about him spread as far as Syria, and people soon began bringing to him all who were sick. And whatever their sickness or disease, or if they were demon possessed or epileptic or paralyzed, he healed them all." (Matthew 4:23-24 NLT).

The big question is why do Christians still get sick? So far in my faith journey (around 43 years at time of writing this book) I have realized that I have a certain amount of personal responsibility for my own personal health. By maintaining a healthy weight and lifestyle I can avoid various diseases and illnesses. Yes, there are still some diseases and illnesses which can be outside of my control but I can work for my physical well-being by sustaining a healthy lifestyle, as far as I am able to.

Up to a year ago, I had a couple of health issues that I was coping with. From a sore lower back, to sore knees while walking, to urinary incontinence from birthing my three sons. After losing forty pounds (eighteen kilograms) I no longer suffer from any of these health issues. By maintaining a healthy weight and daily exercising I have escaped the need for surgery and pain killers. God has given us a wonderful working physical body. We need to look after and nurture it by eating well, daily exercising and making sure that we get a good night's sleep.

Derek Prince, in his book *God's Word Heals* says, "Our lifestyles are built around three things that are not overtly spiritual: diet, exercise and rest. I have come to the conclusion that you cannot expect to be healthy and functioning effectively if you ignore any of those three areas. For example, you can fill your stomach with junk food, but, sooner or later, your stomach is going to rebel. It may take twenty or thirty years, but it will catch up with you. The same is true if you mistreat other areas of your body."[35]

I have also found that sometimes we don't ask for healing; we just try and cope in our own strength. God never wants us to live life on our own terms. He desires us to be dependent on His Spirit living in us. James 4:2 says, "You do not have, because you do not ask." Maybe we don't ask because we feel that our health issues are insignificant compared to others or we have a funny notion that we don't want to bother God. But the Scriptures tell us to cast all of our cares onto Him because He cares for us.[36] If you are feeling doubt about God's desire to heal read the gospels and see how many times Jesus healed people.

What if you are treating your body well and have asked for healing many times but you are still the same? What then? I have a son who has quite bad eczema over most of his body. I thought that once he was in his teen years that he would grow out of it. But no, he is now eighteen and still has to lather himself in creams a couple of times a day. Sleeping is difficult because of the itchiness of his skin. We have tried everything. We have prayed bucket loads of prayers for healing. I don't doubt in God's healing ability. He created my son and knows everything about him. But for some reason God is either saying no or not yet. It's an impairment or weakness that my son has. It affects his work, sleep and relationships with others. I have put this into the same category as Paul's experience with his "thorn in the flesh." Paul defines this as a weakness which he had asked God to take away three times. God answered him each time and said "My grace is all you need. My power works best in weakness."[37] There is a greater working of God's power when we are weak. If we were always strong we would not experience this amazing power. My son has such a lovely empathy for others who are not perfect because he has lived it out in his own life.

I believe that God does want us to be healthy and well, but above everything He desires that we walk by faith, not by sight and live a life totally dependent on Him. This may mean that His grace is enough in a certain situation.

Planet Prayers

This is not praying for the planets. This is praying for people and events on the earth. Our praying influence is not only for our own little personal world or ourselves or our family and friends, but it can reach to cover the whole planet. What an amazing opportunity we have to pray for total strangers and events.

"I urge you, first of all, to pray for all people. Ask God to help them; intercede on their behalf, and give thanks for them. Pray this way for kings and all who are in authority so that we can live peaceful and quiet lives marked by godliness and dignity. This is good and pleases God our Savior, who wants everyone to be saved and to understand the truth." (1 Timothy 2:1-4 NLT).

This was Paul's most important request in his first letter to Timothy, a young pastor, to pray for all people. To ask God to help them. To intercede on their behalf and to give thanks for them. This includes praying for random people, your neighbors, the people in your community, current events, world events and anybody who is in authority such as presidents, your local representative, your mayor or your teacher. This is having a bigger focus -- a God focus -- a planet focus. Not focusing only on our needs, but looking further and seeing the world as God sees it, full of hurting people that need someone to take up the prayer mantle and bring them to the Father. It's an awesome opportunity to partner with God in praying for events and strangers. These people are strangers to you but they are not to God. He created them and also has a plan for their lives.

Praying for Random People

It is easy to be carried away in our own little world and not truly see the people that we come across. There is a reason that they have come across our paths: to share what Jesus has done for us. Most of the time we don't or can't chat with people. We can pray for them. People that we may never even speak with but we can see that they have needs. Random people.

When we start to have a planet focus and think big just like our God is big, we see random people that we come across as real people with real needs. Why don't we pray for them? It doesn't have to take much time. Just shoot a petition prayer to God on their behalf. This is an amazing ministry opportunity, to pray for whoever crosses your path every day. Every Christian can take up this type of prayer ministry.

Most of the time we go through our day without a single thought towards strangers that cross our paths. But God cares for them. Let's follow the example of Jesus as told by Mark in chapter 10. Jesus and His disciples were traveling to Jerusalem. He had just finished telling His followers that He came to serve many, not to be served. As they were leaving Jericho to get to Jerusalem Bartimaeus, a blind beggar, disrupts his travel plans and cries out for the Son of God to have mercy on him. Everyone was trying to get Bartimaeus to be quiet. Fancy calling out like that. Jesus has more important things to do like get to Jerusalem. But Jesus knew the purpose for His life: to seek and save the lost. Bartimaeus was part of the lost. We have lost people everywhere. The girl at the checkout, the neighbor across the road, the petrol pump attendant. **We don't have to travel to Africa to meet the lost for Jesus; they are in our back yard.** What did Jesus do? He asked Bartimaeus what he would like Jesus to do for him. Straight away Bartimaeus asked for the ability to see again. [38]

We have the very Kingdom of God living inside of us. As we share the Kingdom with people that we meet light is shed onto their life path. We have the resources for people to *see*. To "see" their state before an Almighty God. To "see" their need for a Savior. To "see" God's amazing grace-filled eyes filled with love for them. Jesus saw every person as an opportunity to introduce them to the Kingdom of God. Even if we can't say any words to people we come across, we can still pray for them.

Our prayers for random people are effective. It is easy to think that our prayers are only effective for the people that we personally know. Maybe this is because we will probably see the results of our prayers for people we know. Whereas we probably won't come into contact with a random person again. James says, "The prayer of a righteous person has great power as it is working." (James 5:16b). He doesn't say the prayer is only powerful if it is prayed for someone that you know. No, prayer is powerful whether it is for someone we know or for a random stranger.

At the beginning of this year I made a goal to pray effectively for the broken people. This is the year to pray effectively and to see God working. While away on vacation, I received my first opportunity on the 3rd day of this year. Here is my journal entry:

Tuesday 3rd January 2017
Onerahi, Northland
Today I had my first opportunity to pray effectively for broken people - right outside my door. A family parked up near the jetty across the road from where we are staying at the precise moment that I am pondering about how I can pray for broken people. I hear the father yelling at the mother. It goes on for over fifteen minutes. I can't hear what he is so angry about. I see two kids in the back seat looking out of the window. They get out and occupy themselves with throwing sticks into the water. How can they seem so carefree when there is war going on in their car? Maybe this is their normal. Arguing and fighting may be a daily occurrence. I felt the Father's heart for these people. They are strangers to me but I can pray on their behalf - I can pray for my Father to enter into their lives. I prayed for healing of relationships, for peace, joy, forgiveness and hope. I prayed that I will meet them in heaven. I prayed that

things will change for them today. I declared that peace will reign from today onward. Praise God.

What a marvelous opportunity for ministry. I felt like I was part of a bigger picture, part of God's Master Plan. What is His Master Plan? Paul told Timothy what God's master plan is: He wants "everyone to be saved and to understand the truth." (1 Timothy 2:4b). My little prayer was a seed in the life of that family. It was no accident that I noticed and prayed for that family. I believe that prayer will produce results because God is working. I may not see the results until eternity, but they are no less real.

It is like being a secret agent undercover. Our mission, according to Paul's message to Timothy, is to pray for all people, to intercede on their behalf and to give thanks for them. Why? Because God wants everyone to be saved and to understand the truth.

Take Action

Start looking at your day with God's eyes. Who has He bought along your path that you can minister to in prayer as His undercover secret agent? The checkout operator at your supermarket? The driver in the car beside you? The homeless man begging at the shop entrance? What about that little girl crossing the road? We may not know their names but God does. What do you pray? Start with what Paul said was on God's heart: that they be saved and understand the truth. (1 Timothy 2:4). Ask God for what you should pray. You will be amazed with what flows as prayer. I have found many times praying hope for random people. Other times it's healing of relationships. Sometimes it's for them to know and experience God's love and not the world's hate. Every time it's for them to be saved and for me to meet them in heaven.

Praying the News

Watching or reading the news has become a depressing activity of late. Little babies are being killed by their parents. Youth are fighting in the streets. Homes are being invaded. An elderly man is violently attacked because he dared to try and stop vandalism. Natural disasters seem to be happening every day somewhere around the world. Now we have stories of terror happening outside of war zones in cities just like my own. This week, London was visited with terror with five people killed, 40 people injured.

I feel so helpless after reading such painful headlines. I want to fix all the evil in the world. I want help the victims. But what can I do? I will never have enough money, time or skill to help. I have my own family to look after and provide for. I asked God a couple of years ago What can I do? He led me to a book called <u>Praying the News: Your Prayers are more Powerful than you Know</u> by CBN News co-anchor Wendy Griffth and Craig Von Buseck.[39] This book opened up my eyes to the amazing opportunity to pray for the people and events in the news. I no longer felt powerless to help. The book suggests that "as you watch, read or listen to the news, the Holy Spirit will highlight a particular story that He will want you to pray for. If you are able, lift up a prayer at that very moment. God will often put a burden on your heart for a story or a person in the news and will remind you to pray again and again. Yield to the Holy Spirit and intercede for these things until the Lord lifts the burden from you, or the headlines change."[40]

Take Action

Rather than being fearful or feeling powerless to help, pray. Make it a habit of picking one news story a day to pray for the people involved or the area it concerns. It could be a story about out of control youth in a small town or elderly people who have lost their life savings to a con man. Maybe it's praying against the effects of a storm or help for the homeless people in your community. Whatever the current news story is we have a marvelous opportunity to bring God's power into the situation by praying.

Problem Prayers

What would our typical day look like if we lived worry free? Wouldn't it be amazing? It sounds like freedom. Whatever happened in your day you wouldn't be worried about the outcome. Why? Because you knew that your Heavenly Father has your back. The moment a worry thought enters your mind you pass it over to God. It's no longer your thought or concern anymore; your Father is taking care of it.

There is an amazing promise that Paul writes to the Philippians that if we put into practice constantly we would be living a very peaceful life. "Don't worry about anything; instead, pray about everything. Tell God what you need, and thank him for all he has done. Then you will experience God's peace, which exceeds anything we can understand. His peace will guard your hearts and minds as you live in Christ Jesus." (Philippians 4:6-7 NLT).

God wants us to pray about everything. God desires for us to give Him all our worries and for us to live worry free. Worry free living is God's best plan for our lives. We have to do two actions to live worry free.

- Pray about everything. Don't worry. Pray. Tell God what you need.

- Thank Him. This is vital and very powerful. I will share more on this powerful action in the next section.

What does God do? Something big happens: He places a peace guard around our mind and heart, where we think and feel. We can't see His peace guard but He will put in in place as soon as we tell Him what we need. This peace guard comes straight from Him. The Greek word for guard is a military word *phroureo* which means to either prevent a hostile invasion or to keep the inhabitants of a besieged city from flight.[41]

I have found that this peace guard stops any future thoughts or feelings that are not peaceful about that particular situation. It is also extremely effective; people will notice. They will scratch their heads and wonder how you can be so settled in your spirit when your world is turning upside down. You won't even understand why you are so at peace. It's the peace guard God put in place doing its job.

I remember one occasion when I physically felt God's peace guard take up its position. We were in a very tough situation. My husband was in another country looking for work. The kids and I were living with my parents. We had sold most of our possessions and we were going to follow and set up a new life where my husband was working. That was the idea. But there was a series of bad events that stopped that plan. My husband had a serious car accident which used up all our savings for the move over. His work contract ended abruptly due to the company going into receivership. We only had enough money for him to fly home. Now, we were homeless (2 of my sons were living in my parent's garage), had no money and no jobs. I had also been suffering from a severe lower back injury and had been bedridden for a while.

One night I laid it all out before God. I prayed. I cried. I wrestled. All night. I wasn't going to stop until the promise from Philippians 4:6-7 became evident. I was desperate. Then just before dawn I felt a lift in my spirit. The burdens had gone. I physically felt a pouring out of something on my head. It poured down my body all the way to the tips of my toes. It was God's peace guard. I felt like a completely different person. Something spiritual and physical had just happened. In the matter of a couple of months we both were employed in good jobs and then God gave us our home.

Take Action

What would your life look like if you took Philippians 4:6-7 and lived it? Everyday? That is God's best plan for our lives. Decide that from today onward you will take every worry thought, every concern to God, your Father. Even the smallest thing, take it to God. Everything and anything. Nothing is too small or too big. God knows it all, and nothing will shock Him or surprise Him.

Seal your prayer with thanksgiving. Thanksgiving is very important. Thank God for listening and answering. Thank Him for His peace. Then walk out the door with confidence that your Father is taking care of things. He has your back. You can face anything with this knowledge.

What if things aren't improving? What if your situation is still dire? Don't give up. Keep coming to the Father with your worries and needs. Keep thanking Him. Keep believing that "all things work together for those who love God and are called according to His purpose." (Romans 8:28 NET). In the Amplified version the verse says, "And we know [with great confidence] that God [who is deeply concerned about us] causes all things to work together [as a plan] for good for those who love God, to those who are called according to His plan and purpose." (Romans 8:28 AMP).

After praying, your situation probably still looks the same in the visible world, but a massive shift has occurred in the invisible world. God is guarding you with His peace and is at work behind the scenes. Weaving all the bad things - your health issues, your financial problems, your grief and loss - into something good.

The Problem with Problems

We know that our problems are a problem, right? But I wonder whether we truly understand how destructive they can be if they are ignored or not dealt with. Jesus called problems *the cares of the world.* In Mark chapter 4 where Jesus taught about the sower that went out to sow the word, He lumped problems with the deceitfulness of riches and the desires of other things. These three things not only stop the Word from producing something in our lives, they choke the Word.

"But the cares of the world and the deceitfulness of riches and the desires for other things enter in and choke the word, and it proves unfruitful." (Mark 4:19).

The Message version reads "The seed cast in the weeds represents the ones who hear the kingdom news but are overwhelmed with worries about all the things they have to do and all the things they want to get. The stress strangles what they heard, and nothing comes of it." (Mark 4:9 MSG).

Have you ever wondered why you don't seem to be understanding or getting anything from reading God's Word? The stress of your problems strangles the good news that God is trying to bring into your life. God's Word is powerful but if we haven't dealt with our problems then it is rendered useless. Problems stop you from benefiting from hearing God speak through His Word. Problems stop your spiritual growth from taking place. They keep you at the ground floor, not allowing you to move up. It's like being in an elevator and you are pushing the button to move up to the next level but nothing seems to be happening. Maybe the doors are opening and closing but something is stopping the lift from taking off. Problems choke out the Word and your growth.

I believe that we are in the Last Days. Time is getting shorter and shorter till the return of the Messiah, Jesus Christ. What has this to do with problems? In Jesus' teaching on the last days in Luke chapter 21 He mentions a warning to His disciples: "Watch out! Don't let your hearts be dulled by carousing and drunkenness, and by *the worries of this life.* Don't let that day catch you unaware, like a trap. For that day will come upon everyone living on the earth." (Luke 21:34-35 NLT).

The worries of this life will dull our hearts. When our hearts are dull we won't be aware of the times and seasons. We won't be awake and notice the signs that Jesus' coming is imminent. What is a dull heart? The Greek word is *bareo* which means to burden, weigh down and depress.[42] Problems by their very nature weigh us down. They take over our thoughts and affect our emotions. Our hearts become dull. Our eyes are focused on the problem and not on God. We don't see God working things out for good in our life and in the world.

This is a strong warning for our times. Our lives become filled with everyday concerns with no room for God. Our lives are too filled with problems and worries that *that day* may come upon us *suddenly* like a trap. Isn't *that day* supposed to be our homecoming, something glorious? Why would *that day* be like a trap? A trap is something that brings peril, loss and destruction according to Thayer's Greek Lexicon. Problems have the ability, if we let them, to affect what happens on *that day.*

So, what are we to do with problems? I certainly don't want to be caught in a trap when Jesus comes back.

Peter tells us the answer in 1 Peter 5:7 "Casting all your anxieties on him, because he cares for you." I love the Greek word for casting: *epiripto.* Here's how Rick Renner from "Sparkling Gems From the Greek" explains this word: "The Greek word *epiripto,* is a compound of the words *epi* and *ripto.* The word *epi* means *upon,* as *on top of something.* The word *ripto* means *to hurl, to throw* or *to cast,* and it often means *to violently throw* or *to fling something with great force.*[43]"

Have you ever had a large cockroach fall on you? Cockroaches are my nemesis. I hate them. It's hard to escape them in Australia and they grow them big over there. I was reminded of the strong idea of this word *to cast* when I was visiting Australia while in a clothes shop. While unfolding a pair of jeans in the store a giant cockroach jumped out and landed on me. My instant reaction was to fling it off super quickly, no mucking around. Oh, there was probably a scream at the same time. It is the same type of action required for problems, worries and concerns: treat them like a giant cockroach has landed on you. Instantly, without delay, fling them violently onto God in prayer.

Don't Pray the Problem

I find it interesting that Peter doesn't tell us in 1 Peter 5 to talk to God about our problems and worries. What? We don't pray about the problem? Isn't that what petition prayer is all about, praying about your problems? No, we are to cast our cares onto God not talk about them again and again. What is it called when someone is talking about their problems, pains and issues on more than one occasion? Complaining.

Prayer is not telling God your problem. God already knows your problems. What He wants us to do is to chuck the problem over onto Him. He wants us to live worry free and at peace. Does God like to hear us talk about our problems? No one likes to listen to someone going on and on about what is troubling them. Complaining rouses up God's anger. "And the people complained in the hearing of the Lord about their misfortunes, and when the Lord heard it, his anger was kindled, and the fire of the Lord burned among them and consumed some outlying parts of the camp." (Numbers 11:1). Complaining is serious to God, and dangerous to the complainer.

So How Do We Pray?

We throw our cares, worries and problems onto God and then we pray God's solutions. I ask God for His truth of the situation, to see God's reality not our own earthly ideas. I ask God for His Word on the issue. I search the Word for God's solution. Then I talk (a.k.a pray) to God about what His Word says. If I can't find a solution in the Word I wait on the Lord.

"Be still *(wait)* and know that I am God. I will be exalted among the nations, I will be exalted in the earth!" (Psalm 46:10 *emphasis mine*).

While you are waiting stop talking about your problem. Start knowing that God is God. Realize that whatever happens in your life, God will be exalted.

Pray that God will be exalted in your particular situation.

Thanks Daddy!

Every father wants to have children that are grateful. There is nothing more disappointing than a spoiled child who is always putting their hands out expecting good things and not showing appreciation. Why do we think that God is not the same type of father? He has a father's heart that delights in giving good gifts to His children. "Every good gift and every perfect gift is from above," James 1:17. He also feels hurt when we don't express our thanks for what He has provided for us.

I have been studying the book of Ezekiel online with a group of believers and I was astounded by God's intense feelings in chapter 16. God lists out all the blessings that He had bestowed on His children but they ungratefully turned their backs on Him. They even took what He gave them and used it in their idol worship in God's own temple! Including sacrificing their own children, a gift from God. We would never think of carrying out some of the activities that are described in Ezekiel 16, but are we guiltless of not appreciating God and His gifts? Do we worship Him with our whole heart, not just our Sunday personality but in our everyday comings and goings? Is God our number one?

Thanking God Is Seeking God's Kingdom

Thanking and praising God is Matthew 6:33 in action: "But seek first the kingdom of God and his righteousness and all these things shall be added to you." It's a reordering of priorities. Refocusing on God's way of living. When we are seeking His kingdom first, praising and thanking Him would be at the top of our to-do list. It's giving God the glory first. His name honored before our own.

Paul wrote to the believers in Thessalonica about thankfulness and told them to "Give thanks in all circumstances for this is the will of God in Christ Jesus for you." (1 Thessalonians 5:18). Thankfulness is God's desire for His children; it's His purpose for us. If we are wondering what God's will is for us in anything, be it where to live, who to marry or what job to accept, the first step is always thanking God.

Mix Thanksgiving with Petition

Mixing thanksgiving with petition prayers is essential to effective praying. I learned this lesson in 2013 when, as a family, we were going through hard times. While my husband was searching for work in Australia and we were staying with my parents in New Zealand our savings had dried up. While out walking on a September spring morning, I cried out to God for wisdom. I had so many questions running through my head. I tossed and turned throughout the night trying to process what the next step was for us. God, are we to stay in New Zealand or move to Australia? When were we ever to have our own home? What is the next step? I felt stuck in no man's land.

I felt an impression that God desired to give me wisdom more than I wanted it. He showed me what to do while I was waiting for an answer. He showed me the next step, to thank and praise Him. Right there on that crisp spring morning thanking Him was the only action that I could do. While I am waiting for issues to be sorted out, while I am trusting God I can be thanking and praising Him. I realized that every day that I spend praising Him and living from His presence is a day closer to a decision and clarity.

Each day I would make thanking God for everything as my top priority. Most days I wouldn't feel like it. It felt like our situation was dire, but there were still many things that I could thank Him for. My sons were all healthy and well. We still had a roof over our heads at my parents' home. We had three meals a day. We had friends who were supportive. There was always something that I could thank God for. Our situation didn't change overnight but I felt a shift in my spirit. Faith and hope started to bubble up from within. A year later we both gained employment and we moved out of my parents' home into our own home, praise God! The situation wasn't sorted overnight but I was living from a state of peace rather than turmoil. By thanking God daily I was placing my hand into His while He walked us through.

Philippians 4:6, the most famous verse on anxiety, clearly shows the recipe for prayer, to always mix petition prayer with thanksgiving. This combination brings peace. "Don't worry about anything. Instead pray about everything. Tell God what you need, and thank him for all he has done. Then you will experience God's peace, which exceeds anything we can understand. His peace will guard your hearts and minds as you live in Christ Jesus." (Philippians 4:6 NLT). I don't completely understand why this combination is so powerful, but Paul carries on telling us in verse 8 to fix our thoughts on the positive. Fear thrives in negativity, but faith grows in a positive environment. A prayer of faith is filled with thanksgiving.

Gateway to God

Thanksgiving and praise is the gateway into the inner courts in our relationship with God. Psalm 100:4 tells us that thanksgiving is where we start as we travel on our faith journey. "Enter his gates with thanksgiving, and his courts with praise! Give thanks to him, bless his name." As we start our day with thanksgiving, as we start our prayers with thanksgiving, we enter into the place where God is presently working out his purposes. I believe that the more we thank and praise God for all His benefits towards us the more we enjoy the abundant life that Jesus died to give us. Thanksgiving multiplies our joy.

Simple Ways to Give Thanks

The Psalmist in Psalm 92 tells us to sandwich our day praising and thanking God. "It is good to give thanks to the Lord, to sing praises to the Most High. It is good to proclaim your unfailing love in the morning, your faithfulness in the evening." (Psalm 92:1-2

NLT). Why? Because it is good. The Hebrew word for good here is *tov* -this means something that is functioning well.[44] When we give thanks to God we are functioning well. We were created to give God glory and when mankind comes short of His glory sin enters. When you awake make it your first order of the day to give thanks to God for his covenant love (*hesed* in Hebrew) to you. God's covenant love is something no one and nothing can break.

Remind God of His covenant with you and thank Him for everything that covenant means. Sins forgiven past, present and future. The promise of *Immanuel*, God with us, forever. Nothing can separate you from God's love. Then enjoy Jesus' presence during the day. End the day with Him on your mind declaring how faithful He is to you. Turn every circumstance that happened that day into thanks back to Him. Cultivate a lifestyle of thanksgiving.

Praise His Name

Thanksgiving and praising His name go hand in hand. We tend to gloss over the importance of the Lord's name. It is interesting to note that the very first item on Jesus' prayer list in Matthew 6 was hallowed be the name of our Father who is in heaven.

Hallowed is not a word that we use in everyday speech, but the concept of setting something apart and considering it as sacred. Sports is a sacred pastime in my country. We take time out to be a player and/or a supporter. That time is regarded as special and nothing is allowed to disrupt watching or playing the game. How much more is considering God's name as sacred and special. It's at the top of Jesus' prayer list.

Jesus tells us to ask for anything in His name and He will do it (John 14:13-14). So that tells me that Jesus' name is powerful. It sounds like an open check but reading in context we find in verse 12 that Jesus is referring to the works that He did while on earth: preaching, healing, calming storms and providing lunch for over 5,000 people. Anything to do with glorifying God and loving people, Jesus says, ask for it using My name and it will be done for you.[45] What a marvelous promise. With backing like that why do we fret and worry about what little we have? Peter must have remembered this amazing promise when he said to the lame man "I have no silver and gold, but what I do have I give to you. In the name of Jesus Christ of Nazareth, rise up and walk!" (Acts 3:6). Immediately this lame man was lame no more. He leaped up and down praising God. This is a perfect example of using the name of Jesus to glorify God.

Let's daily practice praising the name of the Lord. From the time we wake up let the name of Jesus be our first words. When the sun sets let our thoughts be pondering how His name was glorified that day. "Praise the Lord! Praise O servants of the Lord, praise the name of the Lord! Blessed be the name of the Lord from this time forth and forevermore! From the rising of the sun to its setting, the name of the Lord is to be praised!" (Psalm 113:1-3). Mixing our petition prayers with thanksgiving and praising the name of the Lord is powerful and effective.

God's Word: Daddy, What Do You Think?

Our desire is to pray effectively, isn't it? We want our prayers to mean something. We want to see change and transformation after we pray. We want the extraordinary to take over and transform our situation and the lives of others. In order to pray effectively and see God turn up we need to know what God's thoughts are on the situation. The Word of God, the Bible, is the very thoughts of God. Using the Word of God in prayer is as powerful as wielding a sharp sword.

Eugene Peterson says that "we only pray well if we are immersed in Scripture. It gives you the vocabulary".[46] Beth Moore says, "Praying scripture is not the only means of demolishing strongholds; I've just found it to be among the most effective."[47]

Mademe Guyon, a French believer, wrote a book on prayer titled <u>A Short and Easy Method of Prayer</u> where she shares her belief that one should pray all the time and in whatever one does, one should be spending time with God. She was imprisoned for 8 years after writing this book. Here is her method of using scripture in prayer, in her own words:

"Here's how you should begin.

Turn to the Scripture; choose some passage that is simple and fairly practical.

Next, come to the Lord. Come quietly and humbly. There, before him, read a small portion of the passage of Scripture you have opened to. Be careful as you read. Take in fully, gently, and carefully what you are reading. Taste it and digest it as you read. In the past it may have been your habit, while reading, to move very quickly from one verse of Scripture to another until you have read the whole passage. Perhaps you were seeking the main point of the passage. But in coming to the Lord by means of 'praying the Scriptures' you do not read quickly; you read very slowly. You do not move from one passage to another, not until you have sensed the very heart of what you read.

You may then want to take that portion of Scripture that has touched you and turn it into prayer. 'Praying the Scripture' is not judged by how much you read but the way you read. If you read quickly it will benefit you little. You will be like a bee that merely skims the surface of a flower. Instead, in this new way of reading with prayer, you become as the bee who penetrates into the depths of the flower. You plunge deeply within to remove the deepest nectar. Plunge into the very depths of the words you read until revelation, like a sweet aroma, breaks out upon you.

I am quite sure that if you will follow this course, little by little you will come to experience a very rich prayer that flows from your inward being."[48]

I love to pray this way. I know that the very words that I pray are God's words. When we are confident in what we are praying there is no doubt. James says that when we are full of doubt we shouldn't expect to receive what we pray for. Praying the Word is praying the will of God.

Here are five examples of discovering what God thinks on an issue and praying His words effectively.

1. Daddy, what do you think about my finances?

"Owe no one anything, except to love each other, for the one who loves another has fulfilled the law." (Romans 13:8).

"For where your treasure is, there your heart will be also." (Matthew 6:21).

"Wealth gained hastily will dwindle, but whoever gathers little by little will increase it." (Proverbs 13:11).

Father, I thank you for our jobs. I thank you that we are able to work and provide for our family. I ask Father, that you help us to focus on loving and caring for others rather than the money. Help us to use our money wisely and bring glory to your name. Help us to become debt free so that we owe no one anything

except love. Lord, from you Word you say that it is
better to gather little by little. Please help us in our
savings goal to continue to put aside a portion every
week. Show us when our treasure is money rather
than you.

2. Daddy, how shall I pray for my family?

"Yes Lord, walking in the way of your truth, we wait
eagerly for you for your name and your renown are
the desire of our souls." (Isaiah 26:8).

"Walk with the wise and become wise; associate
with fools and get in trouble." (Proverbs 13:20 NLT).

"The Lord will accomplish that which concerns me;
you [unwavering] lovingkindness, o Lord, endures
forever. Do not abandon the work of your own
hands." (Psalms 138:8 AMP).

Yes, Lord, I pray that my sons walk in the way of your
truth. I pray they wait eagerly for you because your
name and your renown are the desires of their souls.
Please help my sons to be wise and to have wise
friends. I pray that any desire to be associated with
fools will disappear. I thank you Father that what
concerns me concerns you. My children concern me
and I thank that you will complete them and
accomplish your purposes for them.

3. Daddy, what shall I do about this problem?

"God is our refuge and strength, always ready to help in times of trouble." (Psalm 46:1 NLT).

"Count it all joy, my brothers, when you meet trials of various kinds." (James 1:2).

"Blessed be the God and Father of our Lord Jesus Christ, the Father of mercies and God of all comfort, who comforts us in all our affliction, so that we may be able to comfort those who are in any affliction, with the comfort with which we ourselves are comforted in God." (2 Corinthians 1:3-4).

Thank you God for being my refuge and strength right now. Thank you that you are always ready to help me. Please help me now. Help me to be joyful in the middle of this problem. Please comfort me so that I can comfort others.

4. Daddy, I need some guidance about ...

"If any of you lacks wisdom, let him ask God, who gives generously to all without reproach, and it will be given him." (James 1:5).

"Teach me your way, o Lord, that I may walk in your truth; unite my heart to fear your name." (Psalm 86:11).

"Trust in the Lord with all your heart, and do not lean on your own understanding. In all your ways acknowledge him, and he will make straight your paths." (Proverbs 3:5-6).

Father, I need your wisdom and guidance about _____. You promise to give this to me generously without finding fault, and I receive it now. Please teach me your way in this situation, and show me what the truth is. Help my heart (feelings) and my mind be in agreement; not double minded but single in focus. Whatever the decision, help me to always fear your name. Lord, I don't want to rely on my understanding of the circumstances I want your understanding. Help me to trust in you with everything that I am and have. I acknowledge you today please make my path straight today. Thank you Jesus.

5. Daddy, what do you think about my future?

"For I know the plans I have for you, declares the Lord, plans for welfare and not for evil, to give you a future and a hope." (Jeremiah 29:11).

"And I am sure of this, that he who began a good work in you will bring it to completion at the day of Jesus Christ." (Philippians 1:6).

"For this light momentary affliction is preparing for us an eternal weight of glory beyond all comparison, as we look not to the things that are seen but to the things that are unseen. For the things that are seen are transient, but the things that are unseen are eternal." (2 Corinthians 4:17-18).

Thank you for the plans that you have for me, Lord. Thank you that they are good plans for a future filled with hope. Thank you that I can be confident that you are doing a good work inside me and that you will complete that work. Help me to look at the unseen where you are working. Help me to focus on the eternal things and not the temporary.

Take Action

Whatever you want to bring before God in prayer find verses from the Bible that speak about the issue. Then follow Mademe Guyon's method of simple prayer using the Word. Meditate and ponder the verses. Ask God to show you His heart and thoughts on your issue. Then talk to Him using the Word.

CONCLUSION

Seeing the Extraordinary

"God doesn't call us to do extraordinary things, but to do ordinary things with extraordinary love."
- Jean Vanier[49]

This guide is for ordinary people who are seeking the extraordinary in their lives. You may be thinking that there is nothing earth shattering in this little guide. And there probably isn't. As King Solomon wrote, "there is nothing new under the sun."[50] I wanted to show that ordinary people can take the ordinary details of their lives, saturate it in prayer and the extraordinary will turn up.

My prayer for you is to start seeing God as your Heavenly Father, just like Jesus taught us to do with

His simple prayer. Prayer is simple, just like children coming to their daddy for help, to give and receive love and to ask for advice.

My desire is that as you, an ordinary person, who simply prays, may experience God turning up, in all His glory, fashioning the ordinary details of your life into something extraordinary.

Final Take Action

For more helpful articles on connecting with God subscribe to my email list at rachellarkin.com/simpleprayerbonus and receive the bonus material as a reader of Simple Prayer book.

Website: rachellarkin.com
Facebook: facebook.com/RachelLarkin.blog/

If what I have written here has encouraged you in your prayer journey and helped you see God 'turn up' in your day then share this book with your loved ones. Please leave a review on the site where you obtained this book– that helps others hear the message that Prayer is simply us conversing with our Creator Father.

ABOUT THE AUTHOR

Rachel Larkin lives in New Zealand with her husband and their three young adult sons. She writes about growing in faith and developing your potential on her website http://rachellarkin.com/ . She is also a practicing Chartered Accountant, home-schooler for fourteen years and craves chocolate constantly.

FREE EBOOK

To find out more on seeing God turn up in your daily life, Rachel has a free eBook available for download. Get your copy here: http://rachellarkin.com/free-ebook/

NOTES

[1] 1 Kings 17:13-14

2 Exodus 4:2

3 Mears, Henrietta C. Founders of Our Faith: Genesis through Deuteronomy (Tyndale House Pub, 2016) pg 85

4 Murray, Iain; The Early Years (London: Banner of Truth, 1962) pg 87-90

5 http://reasonabletheology.org/the-lasting-impact-of-c-h-spurgeon/ (last accessed 5th May 2017)

6 Renner, Rick. "Sparkling Gems from the Greek" (Teach all Nations 2003)

7 Renner, Rick. "Sparkling Gems from the Greek" (Teach all Nations 2003)

8 http://www.desiringgod.org/messages/meditate-on-the-word-of-the-lord-day-and-night (accessed 21/04/2017)

9 https://billygraham.org/story/notable-quotes-from-billy-graham/ (accessed 21/04/2017)

10 Edwards, Dwight: Releasing the Rivers Within (WaterBrook,2003)

11 Renner, Rick. "Sparkling Gems from the Greek" (Teach all Nations 2003)

[12] Romans 5:8

[13] Renner, Rick. *"Sparkling Gems from the Greek"* (Teach all Nations 2003) page 972

[14] https://www.youtube.com/watch?v=H0rANwWifTE

[15] Moore, Beth. *Praying God's Words* (B & H Books: September 2009) page 5

[16] Moore, Beth. *Praying God's Words* (B & H Books: September 2009) page 6

[17] Piper, Don. *Desiring God: Meditations of a Christian Hedonist.* (Multnomah Books,2015) http://www.desiringgod.org/books/desiring-god

[18] http://rachellarkin.com/2016/09/13/take-a-peek-into-my-one-word-process/

[19] Luke 11:1

[20] Renner, Rick. *"Sparkling Gems from the Greek"* (Teach all Nations 2003)

[21] Lucado, Max. *Before Amen: The Power of a Simple Prayer.* (Nashville: Thomas Nelson, 2014), 9.

[22] Renner, Rick. *"Sparkling Gems from the Greek"* (Teach all Nations 2003)

[23] Lucado, Max. *Before Amen: The Power of a Simple Prayer.* (Nashville: Thomas Nelson, 2014), 7.

[24] Doone, John: Devotions upon emergent occasions and several steps in my sickness- Meditation XVII (1624)

[25] http://www.forbes.com/sites/carolinebeaton/2016/02/25/never-good-enough-why- millennials-are-obsessed-with-self-improvement/

[26] https://www.famousscientists.org/7-great-examples-of-scientific-discoveries-made-in-dreams/

[27] Exodus 35:31; 31:3

[28] Job 28:28, Proverbs 1:7; 9:10; 15:33

[29] John 8:32

[30] https://michaelhyatt.com/5-reasons-why-you-should-commit-your-goals-to-writing.html

[31] http://www.huffingtonpost.com/marymorrissey/the-power-of-writing-down_b_12002348.html

[32] http://www.dictionary.com/browse/mentor?s=t

[33] Hyatt, Michael: Living Forward: A Proven Plan to Stop Drifting and Get the Life You Want (Baker Books: 2016)

[34] Wilson, William. *Wilson's Old Testament Word Studies.* (Massachusetts: Hendrickson Publishers),305

[35] Prince, Derek. *God's Words Heals"* (Whitaker House: 2010)

[36] 1 Peter 5:7

[37] 2 Corinthians 12:9

[38] Mark 10:46-52

[39] Griffth, Wendy & von Buseck, Craig. *"Praying the News"* (Regal: 2011)

[40] Griffth, Wendy & von Busek, Craig. *"Praying the News"* (Regal:2011) page 198

[41] Renner, Rick. *Sparkling Gems From the Greek.* (Teach All Nations: Tulsa, 2003), 323.

[42] Strong's G926 is the root word
(https://www.blueletterbible.org/lang/lexicon/lexicon.cfm?St
rongs=G926 accessed 2nd June 2017)

[43] Renner, Rick : Sparkling Gems From the Greek: 365 Greek
Word Studies for Every Day of the Year to Sharpen Your
Understanding of God's Word (Tulsa: Rick Renner, 2003) pg
325

[44] Benner, Jeff. *The Ancient Hebrew Lexicon of the Bible.* (Jeff
Benner, 2005) AHLB#1186

[45] John 14:13

[46] http://www.desiringgod.org/articles/10-questions-on-
prayer-with-tim-keller

[47] Moore, Beth. *Praying God's Words* (B & H Publishing
Group; 2009) page 9

[48] https://www.ccel.org/ccel/guyon/prayer.html

[49] Vanier, Jean. *Community and Growth.* (Paulist Press, 1989)

[50] Ecclesiastes 1:9

CPSIA information can be obtained
at www.ICGtesting.com
Printed in the USA
LVHW040630010523
745683LV00004B/651